STILL
SMALL
VOICES

STILL
SMALL
VOICES

John and Janet Wallach

With a foreword by
Teddy Kollek, Mayor of Jerusalem

HARCOURT BRACE JOVANOVICH, PUBLISHERS
San Diego   New York   London

For David and Michael

Requests for permission to make copies of any part of
the work should be mailed to:
Copyrights and Permissions Department,
Harcourt Brace Jovanovich, Publishers,
Orlando, Florida 32887.

Library of Congress Cataloging-in-Publication Data
Wallach, John.
Still small voices.
1. Jewish-Arab relations.   2. Palestinian Arabs—
Biography.   3. Israelis—West Bank—Biography.
I. Wallach, Janet.   II. Title.
DS119.7.W336   1989   956   88-32835
ISBN 0-15-184970-6

Endpaper maps by David Lindroth
Designed by G.B.D. Smith

Printed in the United States of America

First edition

A B C D E

But the Lord was not in the wind:
and after the wind an earthquake; but
the Lord was not in the earthquake:
And after the earthquake a fire; but
the Lord was not in the fire: and after
the fire a still small voice.
—1 KINGS 24: 11–12

CONTENTS

FOREWORD . . . . *ix*
    by Teddy Kollek, Mayor of Jerusalem

AUTHORS' NOTE . . . . *xiii*

BORN IN THE REFUGEE CAMP 1
From Prison to the PLO
    Radwan Abu Ayash

THE JEWISH FUNDAMENTALIST 21
Footsteps in the Bible
    Miriam Levinger

THE GAZA STRIP 41
Breeding Ground for the Intifada
    Haidar Abdul Shafi

THE PALESTINIAN GUERRILLA 61
Two Generations of Fighters
    Ahmed Abu Tariq Issawi and Hanni Issawi

THE PALESTINIAN ELITE 77
The Legacy of Leadership
    Faisal Husseini

THE HOLOCAUST SURVIVOR 99
Claiming the Land
    Daniel Cassuto

THE LIBERATION OF THE WOMAN . . . *121*
Mothering the Intifada
  Samikha Khalil

THE JORDANIAN LOYALIST *137*
A Family Divided
  Yasser Obeid

THE ISLAMIC FUNDAMENTALIST *157*
From Moses to Mohammed
  Sheik Bassam Jarrar

THE POLITICIAN *171*
The Risks of Promoting Peace
  Hanna Siniora

THE RABBI OF DIALOGUE *189*
A Bridge to the Future
  Rabbi Shlomo Riskin

ACKNOWLEDGMENTS *209*

FOREWORD

by Teddy Kollek,
Mayor of Jerusalem

For some years, the study, research, and analysis of what is happening in the Middle East have been international pastimes. Innumerable think tanks feed demographic statistics, geographic details, and political exponentials into computers, and we are given a variety of answers as to how our problems can or should be solved, or why they can never be solved.

I do not negate the importance of these activities. But I feel that they ignore the most essential factor, a factor that does not always function as decreed by computer and does not always react according to laws of time and motion. This factor: the people.

In June 1967, following the reunification of Jerusalem, intensive debate ensued. Here were two populations, that of Jew and Arab, who had not only lived on opposite sides of barbed wire and minefields for almost two decades, but who had just engaged one another in war, albeit a short one. There were casualties on both sides. What was the logical next step?

Logic said to wait and move slowly. But despite dire predictions on all sides that a "Belfast" was inevitable, a rather courageous step was taken: on June 28, just three weeks after the cease-fire, we opened the city to both sides.

In one day, people had to learn to live together.

Not to love each other, but to live together. The dire predictions were forgotten as we watched uncertain first steps turn into strides.

What we learned in the following years was that reuniting the city was a task much greater than tearing down antisniper walls and clearing away mines. The greatest challenge was to foster tolerance and neighborly coexistence; we knew it would take unceasing efforts. It was evident that ours would have to be small advances along a very long road: progress would not be a matter of official pronouncements but of teaching people to respect one another, to trust one another.

Reading through this book, I found that the human stories John and Janet Wallach recount lead to perhaps the most meaningful understanding of what is happening today in our part of the world. The problems are problems of people; the solutions will emanate from the people.

I often feel as if our country were not split by a line dividing Arab and Jew, but rather a line dividing extremists and moderates. In *Still Small Voices* one meets Jewish extremists and Arab extremists, Jewish moderates and Arab moderates. As you pass from story to story, so well written, you find your emotions wavering. A solution is possible; a solution is impossible. The Jews are intransigent; the Arabs are intransigent.

At the same time, you feel that the bond shared by both Jew and Arab—their love for this land—is not only one that divides but one that can unite. Both want to live quiet lives and have secure countries in which to raise children and grandchildren.

With all the difficulties, I find Jerusalem to be a microcosm of the possibilities that exist for Jew and Arab to live together. Of course one cannot separate Jerusalem from the rest of the Arab world, and for this reason, in 1967, Jerusalem's Arabs were permitted to keep their Jordanian passports, the Jordanian curriculum in city schools, and their freedom of movement across bridges into Jordan. And yet in Jerusalem, Arabs and Jews meet, work together, share their frustrations in the interminable lines of the government offices, and share their fears as they lie side by side in hospital rooms. Arab and Jewish children attend art classes and film classes and music classes together. While the children are not the ones making the decisions in today's international conferences, they are the ones who tomorrow will have to ensure that Jerusalem is indeed the City of Peace.

AUTHORS' NOTE

For several months beginning in the winter of 1988, we watched, along with most Americans, as the evening news projected horror scenes of battles in the West Bank and Gaza. Night after night, we saw kaffiyeh-clad youths, their faces hooded from the cameras, hurling rocks and gasoline bombs at adolescent soldiers who returned their ire with canisters of tear gas, brutal beatings, and shots of rubber bullets. In the background, television newsmen called out the statistics: two dead here, six hurt there, one maimed over there.

The steady stream of violence seemed to dehumanize the conflict, reducing its victims to abstractions, even taking precedence over the rights being fought for. But as terrifying as the violence was, seldom did we have a sense of who the people were, or why they were so angry, or how it all had started. It was too easy to forget there were human beings on both sides of this bitter conflict.

In writing this book, we hoped to go beyond the stereotypes, to allow the Palestinians and Israelis themselves to tell their own stories and to avoid passing judgment on any of them before we had heard them speak. Beginning with a month-long visit in February 1988, and on a longer stay in the summer of the same year, we lived in the area, meeting with scores of Palestinians and Israelis and listening patiently to their tales. We knew we did not want to put forth a political treatise; instead, we wanted to write a book about the people. Our aim was to go beyond the headlines and television cameras, to reach as far as possible into these people's lives, to find the catalysts for their anger and the causes of their suffering, and in the process begin to peel away the layers of anonymity. We hoped we could at least begin to understand why the problems exist and whether there is any hope of solving them.

There are people who will regard this as a pro-Palestinian book. Others will regard this as a pro-Israeli book. It is not intended to be either. Above all, we hope that readers will see this as a book about human beings who all believe deeply in the righteousness of their cause. And if by the end of the book the reader feels some sympathy for each of them—Arab and Jew—perhaps it will be easier to understand why the conflict is so complex and heart-wrenching.

The people we have chosen to portray live their lives in extraordinary circumstances amid the constant threat of danger in the belief that their very existence in these circumstances is what gives meaning to their lives. This is true of both the Arabs and the Jews.

Both peoples claim an exclusive right to the same land. In deciding how many Palestinians and Israelis to include, we were guided by the fact that there are more than one and a half million Arabs and seventy thousand Jews in the West Bank and Gaza.

We included Israelis for whom the decision to settle in this disputed area was an affirmation of their personal experience and religious commitment. Nevertheless this remains essentially a Palestinian story: it is the Palestinians who lack a homeland, who are denied civil rights, and who are dying in the *intifada*, the uprising against the Israeli occupation.

Before we chose the Palestinians for this book, we

interviewed dozens of Arabs, crisscrossed the roads
from Hebron to Nablus to Gaza, visited remote villages, and spent long days in the refugee camps. We
sipped hundreds of cups of thick Turkish coffee and
ate endless slices of watermelon as we talked with
youngsters, adults, and the elderly. Our aim was to
gain a sense of where they had come from, what they
feared and what they hoped for, and how they lived
their lives. As we drove in cars with blue Arab license
plates we learned the sense of occupation: the checkpoints, the army jeeps, the soldiers on the rooftops
all became a threat. How different it was when we
rode in yellow-plated Israeli cars along the same roads
to the fortified settlements. Suddenly, it seemed, those
very same soldiers were there to protect us. And as
we drank hundreds of cups of filtered coffee and dozens more slices of watermelon we heard the Israelis'
stories too: their fears, their hopes, their traumas.

Those we finally decided to include in the book
all live in the West Bank and Gaza. They represent
several generations, a range of socioeconomic backgrounds and occupations, and a broad spectrum of
opinion—from those considered terrorists, to extreme
religious fundamentalists, to moderate pragmatists.
Although the Palestinians reflect the mainstream of
Arab thinking both in and outside the West Bank, the
Israelis living in the territories do not, by and large,
reflect the majority of opinion inside Israel. Nevertheless, as demonstrated in Israel's 1988 elections,
their claim to Judea and Samaria is supported by more
than a third of the Israeli people.

Working on this book was a continuing challenge
as the *intifada* literally put roadblocks in our way.
Towns and villages were cut off by checkpoints; refugee camps were under curfew; institutes were closed
by military order. We never knew whom we would
be able to interview, because influential Palestinians
were constantly in and out of prison. Fortunately, two
key figures, Faisal Husseini and Radwan Abu Ayash,

in prison in February, were released from lengthy sentences by the time we came back in June.

Returning home with Radwan allowed us to witness his emotional reunion with his mother and father. But getting to the refugee camp was not so easy. On two occasions we had made appointments with Radwan to drive to Nablus. As we read in the morning papers of new casualties of the *intifada*, we argued over whether or not to cancel. But minutes later, on each occasion, the phone rang: Radwan could not make it. Only later did we learn from him that he had been informed there probably would be violence and it would be safer to stay away.

It was easier to get to El Bireh to see Samikha Khalil. We made our appointment a week in advance, but by the time we arrived, the doors of her institute had been welded shut. She was surrounded by consoling friends and was concerned that she would now be put under arrest.

We made several efforts on Friday afternoons to hear Bassam Jarrar, an Islamic sheikh, deliver his lecture in various mosques. Soldiers at hastily constructed checkpoints stopped us and made us turn back. Fridays, it seems, were the days when the sheikhs incited their audience to confront the Israelis.

The drive to Gaza to meet Haidar Abdul Shafi posed no problem. We had been cautioned beforehand not to drive through explosive Gaza City in a car that carried yellow license plates. Therefore, we arranged to be met by a guide south of the city on Route 4 at Yad Mordecai, a rest stop frequented by Israeli troops. But no one was there to meet us. When we called, we were informed that most of the city was under curfew and our Palestinian guide could not get out.

After more than an hour, he arranged to have a taxi with gray Gaza plates bring us to Haidar's house. After the interview, we wanted to meet victims of the *intifada* at Ahali Hospital. But the road was blocked by barbed wire and Israeli troops, and we knew that they would not let reporters through. It took a lot of persuasion and a few white lies to talk our way past the patrol and enter the hospital grounds. Afterward, as we reached the taxi, parked a hundred yards from the soldiers, we heard them yelling to us to return for interrogation. But we quickly left, weaving our way through deserted streets in an effort to find the route that would take us safely out of the curfewed maze. As we drove on the empty road out of Gaza, we passed hundreds of trucks laden with produce lined up at the checkpoint, waiting to get back in.

Faisal Husseini was not so far away. We had seen him several times since his release from prison, first at the Arab Studies Society, then at his home. On our last visit, on a Saturday morning, we asked for an English version of his father's well-known song about the Palestinian struggle.

"Call me on Wednesday," he said, "and I'll have it translated for you."

Concerned that some new obstacle might be thrown in our path, we pleaded for the copy then and there. But Faisal was too busy: waiting in the next room was the Spanish consul-general and an aide.

"Okay," we said, "we'll call the office on Wednesday."

Two days later, the newspapers carried front-page headlines about Faisal's latest arrest. The Arab Studies Society had been ordered closed for a year and he had been taken away, his hands cuffed and his feet shackled, to serve yet another prison term. We never received the song.

As we completed the interviews, Jordan's King Hussein moved boldly to change the political balance, all but eliminating the possibility of some kind of Israeli-Jordanian condominium that excluded the PLO. By severing its ties to the West Bank, administrative and legal, Jordan sent a clear message to Israel that the Jewish state could not maintain its claims to sovereignty without incurring increasing dangers in governing its unwilling inhabitants. Equally, the Jordanian move sent a message to the PLO that the time had come for it to shoulder the political responsibilities incumbent with its claim to be the "sole and legitimate" representative of the Palestinian people. As we finished the book, the Palestine National Council moved closer than ever before to accepting Israel's right to exist, but still stopped short of any explicit recognition, conditioning its acceptance on the establishment of a Palestinian state.

The results of the November elections in Israel strengthened the influence of the right-wing religious parties. The Palestinians, at their meeting in Algiers, declared their independence and asserted the right to establish a state, setting the stage for intensified conflict and increasing the challenge to any American peacemaker.

But regardless of what happens in the political process, these are the people who will have to live together and ultimately make peace with each other. Among them are Palestinians who could emerge as figures of authority in a Palestinian homeland. Sadly, their small voices are stilled by the Israeli government here and by the PLO leadership abroad. The voices of the Israeli settlers are muffled by their terrifying image as armed vigilantes, underscoring the reality that no peace will be possible until they are heard. The cries of each group ring out in fear and hate.

At the time of this writing, the PLO has unilaterally declared an independent Palestinian state, and its chairman, Yasser Arafat, has accepted the United States' conditions for a dialogue: recognition of Israel's right to exist, renunciation of terrorism "in all its forms," and acceptance of UN Security Council Resolutions 242 and 338 that call for all states in the region to have "secure and recognized" borders. While the US has begun a dialogue, the new national unity government in Israel continues to reject talks with the PLO.

Regardless of what happens in the political process, it is the people in this book who will ultimately have to live together and make peace with each other. But for now, cries of both Palestinians and Jews continue to ring out in fear and hate, drowning out the small voices of hope and reason.

Although we cannot offer the coffee and the watermelon, the bumpy rides or the blazing heat, we hope that the reader will take the same journey we took in an effort to understand why both Palestinians and Israelis are fighting so fiercely for what they believe.

—Mishkenot Sha'ananim

STILL
SMALL
VOICES

BORN IN THE
REFUGEE CAMP

From Prison to
the PLO

Radwan Abu Ayash

The head of the Arab Journalists Association in the territories and managing editor of Al-Awdah *magazine, Radwan Abu Ayash, has been put in administrative detention for six months. He was arrested late Tuesday night at his Ramallah home, and is being held at the central West Bank prison at J'neid. The Nablus military court is to hold a hearing today to confirm the order.*

Military sources said Abu Ayash, 37, is "a senior Fatah activist in the West Bank and Jerusalem" who had extensive contacts with Fatah activists in the region and abroad. The sources said his activities included "receiving instructions and funds to promote the organization's aim and to disrupt public order."

—Jerusalem Post, DECEMBER 10, 1987

Hey you guards
Why are you looking at me like this?
We are imbeciles waiting for the morning
This morning is not too far
Even behind the bars
We believe that we are living in the sun.
          —RADWAN ABU AYASH, PRISON SONG

"It was nearly midnight when I heard a very hard knock on the door of my flat. I had just come back from Nablus, the place where my parents live in a refugee camp, and I was in bed with my wife trying to sleep. I came out quickly in my pajamas and heard a voice say, 'We are the police. Open!' When I opened the door I saw about fifteen soldiers, and one of them was a policeman I had known during my six months of town arrest in 1984. 'What do you want?' I asked them, and this very smart one I knew, a tall, handsome man with glasses said, 'You are under arrest.' 'Why?' I asked. 'Because you are PLO.' So I told him, 'There are two million people in the occupied territories who are pro-PLO. You will have to arrest them all.'

"My four children were in the apartment. Suna, she's thirteen; Shadi, he's nine and very bright; Samoud, she's seven and was born when I was in prison and Beirut was under siege, so my wife called her this name which means 'steadfastness'; and Sheda, she's one year old and her name means 'the fragrance of flowers.' Because they were sleeping, I asked the soldiers to be quiet and not wake them but to wait outside. One soldier followed me to my bedroom where I put on my clothes. I told my wife to tell the children in the morning that I was driving to my parents in Nablus to say hello, and then I left with the soldiers. Downstairs there were so many trucks and soldiers, I thought I must be in southern Lebanon.

"I was driven to the military government headquarters in Ramallah, where I was kept for a while. At two A.M. I was put in the back of a transit car, and a few minutes later two guys who were handcuffed and blindfolded were thrown into the back, too. The car drove down the Jordan Valley to Adam's Bridge on the River Jordan, and for a while I thought for sure they were going to deport me to Jordan, that place where they don't like me very much. But at three A.M. we arrived at the detention camp called Farra Jail, near Nablus. They dropped off the two guys and then took me away to Nablus, to the J'neid Prison, the central prison of the West Bank. But the officer who was responsible that night refused to accept me. So they took me back to the military headquarters in Ramallah, where I was kept in the car without food, without water, without anything till ten A.M. Then the same thing happened again. They put in some guys and we drove all the way to Farra, and I began to feel like I was a taxi service. I arrived at J'neid, a five-star Intercontinental compared to the prisons in the Negev, at one o'clock in the afternoon.

"I was made to expose myself like a stripteaser and then was given two plastic plates, a plastic spoon, four blankets, and something they called a pillow. I was taken to a ward of thirty rooms and put in one of the rooms, which hold between eight and sixteen prisoners. There were iron bunk beds with sponge mattresses and not enough space between the top bunk and the bottom to stretch your back. The bathroom, with a toilet and a makeshift shower, was inside the room, so there was no space even to change your clothes in privacy. The room itself was too small to have five people sit and play backgammon. So most of the time people lay on the beds, reading or talking to each other.

"At seven-thirty in the morning we would have to wake up and stand in a circle inside the cell while an officer counted us. Then they would give us breakfast—one egg, which I knew was an egg only because I could see that it was, one spoonful of jam, and a loaf of bread to last for three meals. An hour or so later we were taken outside and allowed to walk for fifteen minutes at a time in the high-walled courtyard. Ten of us would walk together under the barbed-wire sky, getting dizzy from the blinding light and the slanted ground, and after fifteen minutes we had to stop. We would take turns and do this for two and a half hours, then go back inside behind the barbed-wire doors.

"For lunch they gave us soup—hot water and margarine—and something else I could not recognize. At one point, during Pesach, the holiday when the Israelis don't eat bread for eight days, they gave us our allotment of bread for the whole eight days together. Of course, we did not have refrigerators inside the prison, so we put the bread in a blanket in order to keep it cool. After two days it had rotted completely, but we had to eat it. We had no choice; it was either eat or starve, so we ate the rotten bread.

"At night or in the morning sometimes, they would come and drag some prisoners from the cell. The whole ward would begin to sing a song: 'Yes, we will not die; we will stay in our land; our roots are deep; you are trying to uproot us.' No one knew where the prisoners were going, but later we would find out they were deported.

"Our relatives were permitted to visit for half an hour every two weeks. I saw my wife and my children, who had been told about my imprisonment the very next morning by their teachers, but they wouldn't let me see my baby. I went on a hunger strike and fought about this until finally, when I had only one month to go, the soldiers carried the baby in and I could hold her.

"We were allowed to have radios, which we bought from the prison canteen, but most of the time we did not have batteries to make them work. When we did, we listened to the news and discussed it, talking about the *intifada* or about King Hussein. We had a very well organized society, and if you compared it with the outside, you found you were in a real school of thought. It was a school of uprising, a school of spirit, a school of hope.

"We read a lot and had lessons; people who wanted to learn English or Hebrew or physics would find one of the prisoners to teach them. And we would have political discussions at night. The communications were superb. If you wanted something to be known, you hid a note in a cigarette box—God, the cigarettes were awful—and passed it from cell to cell, then from ward to ward, and then it was transported by laborers from yard to yard. Within five minutes the whole prison can know anything you want. I wrote a long song about the guards watching us and our living in the sun. In a few days everybody in the prison knew the words, and they would sing it all the time.

"At one point they brought me to the military judge. They accused me of being a senior activist in the PLO, but this is not true. They had evidence in what they call the secret file—clippings from papers, writings, records of my meetings with people, public statements I had made about things like the Iran-Iraq war—but they wouldn't let me or my lawyer see it. I told the judge, 'Listen, man, for God's sake, tell me what's the charge. If you tell me what's the charge, I'll accept the punishment, and when I come out I will be very dovish. Just let me know.' But he said, 'I can't tell you. This is secret.' They didn't convict me.

"Then after six months they came for me one night, and I thought I was going to be deported. They took me out of the cell and everybody was singing. I didn't know where I was going or what would happen. And then they told me I was free."

ALIENATION TILL VICTORY

My identity is a sack
In this sack are some of my sad memories
Some of my dreams

Some of the deathbeds
And a song to my mother.
And the way of love moves me from the land to
*   the sea*
And takes me to the dark nights looking for the
*   rest of patience*
Looking for my sun and my dawn.
Following me are sultans, sun guards, slammed
*   doors, iron bars and heavenly names*
And the slaves of the king carrying me from stone
*   to stone.*
Behind the stone there is another stone.
That holds in its abdomen
Some of the aroma of tranquillity
And the sad memories carrying the birds of thunder
Again and again, three times, four times, ten times
And the way of love takes me from the sea to the
*   sea*
My sad memories
And some of the deathbeds
And home to my homeland.
    —RADWAN ABU AYASH, from *Violin Melodies*

The ride from his apartment in Ramallah to the refugee camp in Nablus is as familiar to Radwan Abu Ayash as the black beard and black mustache that adorn his dark-skinned face. He drives his white General Motors Opel confidently along the open stretches past the town of El Bireh, where he once taught English at the high school; past the Al-Amari refugee camp, the first of four along the way; past Bet El, the military headquarters and computer center for the West Bank. Just behind it his piercing eyes pick out a settlement and he notes, "We can differentiate between the Arab villages and the settlements by two things: by the mosque and by the road that leads to the place; if it's a horrible road, it's an Arab village; if it's a smart, wide road, it's a settlement."

Huge beige hills sprawl across the landscape, while in the foreground fruit trees bearing olives, grapes, and apricots stretch up from the dusty earth. On the side of the road two little boys call out to passing cars to buy fresh figs from their basket. Farther on, a dozen or so donkeys wait in the fields as women, covered in cloth from head to toe, work in the suffocating heat, their bodies bent to gather wheat, shaft by shaft, in the manner of their ancestors a thousand years before. "This is communism, real communism," sneers Radwan, who once avowed its theories.

For miles around one sees land owned and farmed by Arab villagers; land whose claims lie so deep in the layers of Islam and the traditions of foreign rule that its formal ownership is difficult to trace; land never registered when the Jordanians ruled here because the Palestinians would have had to pay heavy taxes on it; land that now the Israelis might brazenly claim because there are no deeds to it. Here and there, a modern settlement, indomitable symbol of the Israeli occupation, rises above the fields. "They build their settlements like the Romans built their castles—high up on the hills," Radwan says. "This shows you their insecurity."

He takes a side turn and drives to Bir Zeit, a Christian town that boasts the most well known university on the West Bank. Funded by the Saudis and outside Palestinians, it is considered by the Israelis to be a breeding ground for the PLO. This sprawling college for twenty-five hundred students was a major site of action in the early stages of the *intifada*, but the military has long since shut it down. The roads to Bir Zeit are an obstacle course of rocks, burned-out tires, and broken glass from gasoline bombs— remnants of the violence that took place here some months ago. In the town itself, where two women dressed in western-style clothing stroll the sidewalks, the walls are covered with graffiti. Letters painted in red and black—two of the colors of the Palestinian flag—shout in Arabic, "Long live the PLO," "Long live the intifada," "Down with occupation," and "Yes to national unity." The town is silent now, but the anger and the bitterness and the energy of its youth remain so clearly evident.

Radwan shifts gear as the car returns to the main road and begins a winding, steep ascent. Generous mountains yield to gracious valleys, and he points out the spectacular vistas that might someday be Arab cities. About three fourths of the way to Nablus, a rest stop comes into view, and he pulls the car off to the side of the road. The shop inside greets tourists with a chance to buy an ice-cold drink or to choose from an array of souvenirs. Colorful baskets woven of wheat line the shelves, and standing next to them are carved wooden camels, metal menorahs, and decorative plates that say, "Shalom, Y'all." An American tries to bargain over a basket and the Arab owner says, "If you really want it, the price is five shekels. But if you want to bargain, I'll tell you the price is ten shekels and then we'll settle on eight!"

The drive continues, and Radwan tells his guests to put away their notebooks and their pens. "Better not to have them at the checkpoint," he warns. Thirteen kilometers from Nablus, an Israeli flag sticks out of the ground and a series of metal barriers block the road; beneath them rows of metal spikes make sure no one will pass. A soldier waves on the car, in spite of the blue license plate that marks it Arab, but a second soldier flags it down. Speaking in Hebrew, Radwan argues coolly that the first one let him go, but the Israeli is not persuaded. "Never mind. Your identity papers," he says. The Palestinian pulls out his leather carrying case from the glove compartment and shows his documents stamped "State of Israel." "Okay," says the soldier and waves him on. "I never am afraid of them," says Radwan. "I am scared of a bullet coming at me, but not of them. I refuse with all my heart to let them have the right to scare me. They are human beings just like me."

The car speeds along the open road, past more planted fields and ugly camps: past the Nablus prison, where a star of David is emblazoned on the old Jordanian building; past a sign for Joseph's tomb; past the infamous Balata camp, where Molotov cocktails have been thrown at soldiers, and several youths have been killed in return. For days at a time Balata has been under curfew, no residents even permitted to leave their homes, and the exits to the road are blocked by rows of heavy barrels.

At Askar, the crowded refugee camp where he was born in a tent, Radwan turns in at the entrance, marked only by a shabby United Nations Relief Works Association building. Those who live here need no sign to tell them they are home, and strangers don't come by just perchance. He drives his snappy car along the crumbling streets no one has bothered to name and goes by seedy schools shut down on military orders because students threw their rocks at soldiers once too often. Save for the sound of the tires crunching stones, an eerie silence stills the atmosphere; the squalor of the overcrowded barracks appalls the mind, and the stench of sewage overwhelms the senses. Here and there a child bikes by, oblivious to the putrid smell, and one boy wears a yellow T-shirt that proclaims, "It's better in the Bahamas." A few barefoot tots carry a pail of mud packed with filthy water from an open pipe. Radwan, now a model of West Bank success, recalls his own time spent in the playgrounds made of muck and talks about the scraps of wire that were his toys. "I never had a childhood," he says, and adds that now, when he brings a doll home for his children, he takes a few moments first to play with it himself.

The concrete huts that serve as houses for five thousand people press together, endless rows of faceless blocks with holes cut out for windows, symbols of the faceless souls who live here. Broken strips of corrugated tin seal off some blighted lots. Laundry hangs enmeshed with TV antennas on asbestos roofs, and the charred remains of a Palestinian flag are still strung above the road. Loudspeakers dot the camp, connected to the main mosque in Nablus, where a satellite dish mounted by the minaret makes sure that the daily calls to prayers by the muezzin can be heard and the daily calls to action by the *intifada* leaders can be heeded. Life is far better here than it was when the Israelis first took over. Refrigerators, televisions, and telephones are now expected items of possession, symbols of the 1970s prosperity that came with jobs in Israel or from money sent by family members working in the oil-rich Arab states. The harder times of the eighties, caused by Israel's own economic troubles, plus the layoffs resulting from the oil glut, have added to the bitterness of those who live here, feeding the fires of the *intifada*.

The thirty-thousand-dollar car comes to a stop, and a group of children gather to inspect it. "This way," calls the small, slim Radwan proudly, strutting down a narrow path of rubble toward his house. Single file, the visitors make their way along a row of cavelike huts, past an open doorway that reveals a mother and her children huddled in a circle on the ground. The foul odor of sewage and burning kerosene mixes with the food they cook in traditional Arab style on a small open fire.

Radwan, looking natty in his well-cut safari suit, hurries toward a green tin door and greets his teen-aged sisters waiting shyly at the entrance. Inside, an old woman, wrapped in white with checked pajamas underneath, grins from ear to ear and hugs her son as if he were a hero-king come home. The barren room they stand in, filled with the rancid stink of human waste, was a gift from UNRWA nearly forty years ago. But as the family grew in size, Radwan explains, they enlarged the structure until there was space enough to squeeze in all nine children, plus his parents—not a large family by Askar standards. He points to the tile-floored living room that has been added on and compares it with pride to the concrete hole that was the original room from UNRWA. He boasts that his family and friends built it block by block: "We have something called collective help. The minute you start to do something, you'll find somebody is coming to help with the work. This is the spirit of the camp."

A gracious host, he urges his guests toward a yellow-covered divan and offers cold drinks in glasses trimmed with a bird motif. An electric fan tries uselessly to cool the stifling room, its churning motion bringing only more waves of fetid air. A 1950s-style credenza, filled with family photos and cans of plastic flowers, stands against one wall; a dressing table opposite holds copies of *Othello*, and *The Prairie*, strangers from another land mixed in with several shelves of yellowed books in Arabic. A dust-covered television that once must have worked rests in a corner on the floor, a status symbol not to be removed.

When lunch is served—a feast of roasted chicken, saffron rice with pine nuts, spiced meatballs in sauce, tomato salad, and pita bread—the family disappears. Later they will bring huge bowls filled with fruit and serve thick Turkish coffee to the guests. They will eat the leftovers when no one is around.

For Radwan the house is a haunt of miserable memories: hauling rationed food from UNRWA to the huts; hoping desperately for a tip of half a piaster; wading barefoot through pools of mud in melted snow; walking five miles to school and watching hungrily while others munched a sandwich. And yet he speaks with pride of Askar, pointing out its warmth and communality. "You feel here that you're at home and everybody is very close," he says. How different, he notes, "from cities like Amman or in the United States. There, everybody's talking about themselves and nobody cares what you say."

He is clearly satisfied that he has risen from these

slums and reached a position of some respect. As a well-known journalist who speaks for the mainstream Fatah, he has earned himself authority. Asked if a trip he made to the United States was criticized by the radicals, he laughs and shakes his head. "After all," he adds, "I am the one who makes public opinion." As a writer, he is well paid by the pro-Fatah group; his salary, he says, is sixteen hundred dollars a month, a substantial sum by Israeli standards, and enough to live well, drive a new car, and pay for his four brothers' college education. But his ties to Fatah go deeper—deep enough, in fact, that he was chosen as one of four to meet with the foreign minister of Japan in east Jerusalem in the summer of 1988. Though he will not admit to rumors that his car was a present from the PLO, he pauses, then boasts laughingly, "If I asked the PLO for a new car, they would give me better than that—they would give me a truck!"

And yet for forty years his family has lived here in the filth and the mud and the stench and the sickness, claiming to be far from home, waiting to be returned to their house near the sea in Jaffa, only sixty miles away; refusing to accept the Israelis' offers of better housing elsewhere or even of improvements in the camps. True, the camp is wretched, with its open sewers that spread disease, its dirt alleys that turn to seas of slop in the rain, its concrete hovels that are supposed to be homes. But if they left, they ask, where would they go? Who would they be? The camp has truly been their refuge: living here they could claim their old homes; living here they could keep their identity cards; living here they could wait for the Arabs to return their land. Once they leave, they have no claim to anything, not even to the hope of return. "The camp has become a symbol of national identity for every Palestinian refugee. That's why they are sticking to their camps," says Radwan. "*Al-awda*" ("return to the homeland") has been their cry. Yet for Radwan, the reality dawned twenty years ago, when, he says, he learned that the promises and the slogans were nothing more than lies fed to the Palestinians by other Arabs.

It was June 1967, a hot summer day, and Radwan Abu Ayash could barely catch his breath as he ran from the refugee camp to the main road to see the foreign troops marching into Nablus. He stopped at the fence of the Jordanian army's stables; from there the slight eighteen-year-old could watch the troops moving from the mountains of the Jordan Valley toward the old Arab town. All around him people were running and rejoicing, and he joined in the celebration, singing and dancing for the soldiers who had come to liberate Palestine. No one knew which Arab country the army was from—was it Iraq? Algeria? Morocco?—but never mind. What did it matter? Radwan was puzzled too, even more so as he caught a glimpse of a blue-and-white flag painted on the cannons. No Arab country that he knew had such a flag, but he would check his atlas just to make sure. He walked home to Askar and took down the reference book, but nothing in its colorful pages resembled what he had seen. Then suddenly he knew: this was not the army of an Arab nation that had come to free them; this was the army of their enemy, Israel. Now in the background he could hear voices blaring through loudspeakers, enemy voices telling the people to raise up white flags on their houses; within minutes Askar would become a sea of white.

Neighbors prepared to leave, packing their clothes and belongings, but his parents refused, not wanting to flee as they had before in 1948, when they rushed from their home near Jaffa to take shelter here. No, they would stay and pray that an Arab country could still save them. Didn't the other Arabs owe it to them? Hadn't they promised all along that they would destroy Israel and give back to the Palestinians all their land, from Haifa to Jaffa and more? They could not leave the camp. They had to stay and wait for help. They had to claim their status as refugees.

For the first days of the Israeli occupation Radwan moved only in fear, terrified as air force planes buzzed the area of Nablus, dropping pamphlets from the sky. The planes flew so low that the noise of the engines cracked the walls of the concrete huts. At any minute, the boy thought, Askar would become a mass grave. He and his younger brother Adnan went outside and hid under a tree; better to die outdoors, they thought, than to be inside. Leaflets were dropped on the camp, carrying instructions to the people to stay silent, to stay at home, and to shut their doors.

As the week progressed Radwan became angry, first at the Israelis for their conquest, then at the Arabs for his lack of education. Why should I be ignorant? he thought. Why have I not learned about this powerful country, Israel? In his school Israel was not to be mentioned. In his books the Israelis were a small bunch of gangsters whom a few Palestinian youths could put in a boat and push out to sea. Every day he heard the platitudes of Jordan's King Hussein, achieving nothing for the Palestinians and demanding their loyalty in return. He watched the Israeli army and compared it with the Jordanians. How different these working Israeli soldiers were from the showy Jordanian horsemen with their shiny shoes and their circus acrobatics! "The Israeli generals did not care about twinkling boots. They cared about how to get things done. They didn't care about appearances; they had their shirtsleeves rolled up and they were working." It was then, he says, "I began to discover they had built walls in my mind, and every wall was falling."

Radwan's days at Jahez High School in Nablus revealed another world. The city of fifty thousand people was a far cry from the impoverished refugee camp; lush palm trees lined the streets, fresh produce abounded in the stores, and the pages of new books filled his mind. Hungrily, he devoured the words of Marx and Engels and absorbed the slogans of Egypt's Nasser. "Coming out of a very poor community, being aware of other environments, you search for a theory that applies to you," he explains. "I thought communism would be helpful in order to get rid of the situation." The positive side of Soviet influence was apparent in neighboring Egypt, where Russian aid was helping the Egyptians to build the Aswan Dam. Defying the Jordanians, who declared it illegal to follow either communism or Abdel Nasser, Radwan would lie in bed at night and listen to Egyptian broadcasts, his radio hidden under the pillow; Nasser's words seemed to ring with truth. The Egyptian leader called for a pan-Arab nation, an enticing idea that would join together all the Arabs in a united entity and, in the process, eliminate the state of Israel.

But the young student began to turn against the shibboleths of the Arab world when he entered the Teachers Seminar in Ramallah, a training school for educators and, says an Israeli official, "a training ground for agitators." As an English teacher, he became aware that the problems of the Palestinians were deeper than he had thought. "Our people were not only poor, but they were uneducated and did not have a global view. They were looking at things very narrowly." Radwan became convinced that the first priority of the Palestinians had to be education. "We had to have an open mind. We should get rid of all these bloody slogans which were like morphine given to us by the Arab leaders." He discovered that religion, too, fostered the myths, and says that now he doesn't bother with the rituals of Islam.

In the years that followed, Radwan mixed teaching and writing and, in the manner of everything Palestinian, interlaced them both with politics. When asked when he became politically active, he replies, "I joined journalism in 1975." That was the year he began to work for *A-Sha'ab*, a pro-PLO daily and the third-largest newspaper on the West Bank and Gaza. A few years later, he went to teach at Bir Zeit, the most western thinking university on the West Bank. He became more active in the pro-Fatah movement and organized groups in the Shabibah—pro-Fatah youth clubs formed for Palestinian social work and anti-Israeli agitation. He also translated *The Breakthrough*, a book by Moshe Dayan about the Egyptian-Israeli peace treaty, and wrote several books of his own, including *Violin Melodies*, a collection of poems.

In 1979 Radwan became a full-time journalist. His work with the Palestine Press Service, a pro-PLO wire service for newspapers, and his work for *Al-Awdah*, a pro-PLO weekly news magazine, enabled him to keep the Palestinian problem in the public consciousness. Not only did he write articles on self-determination, Palestinian identity, and steadfastness under Israeli occupation, but he served as a guide for the foreign press, feeding them stories that helped stoke the fires of the PLO. In one instance in 1985, when a Palestinian was found dead in the fields of Beit Haron, Radwan created a smooth news campaign. The story, he told the foreign journalists, was that the man had been inspecting some land that an Arab "collaborator" had sold to the Jews and that he had been killed in the field by settlers. But Israeli agents learned the Palestinian had been part of a complex network smuggling weapons into the West Bank. The explosives had been carried into the country by one man, then hidden in the field by someone else; when a third man had gone to find them at the drop point, he had been blown to bits: a Russian F1 hand grenade had exploded in his hand.

It isn't only the Israelis who find Radwan's work threatening. His outspokenness has also put him in trouble with the Jordanians. In 1976, after the PLO split with Jordan, Radwan openly criticized Hussein. The Jordanians responded by placing his name on their blacklist and no longer allowed him to cross the Allenby Bridge into the kingdom.

The cost of being on the blacklist is very high. Like all Palestinians who live on the West Bank, Radwan can leave the area only with his Jordanian passport; but now that is no longer possible. In the past he enjoyed the luxury of traveling to England, France, and Italy—trips that he says helped him further the Palestinian cause. The Israelis say he used them for meetings with PLO leaders, who gave him instructions and money for mobilizing the Palestinians inside the territories.

But even the Israelis could not refuse Radwan permission to travel when American officials invited him for a tour. In 1986 he spent a month as a guest of the United States Information Agency, an arm of the U.S. government, traveling across the country from New York to California. Clutching his Israeli "laissez-passer," he traveled to New York, Washington, Miami, Nebraska, and San Francisco. "I loved Miami," he says. "It gives you the impression of the Mediterranean, and I like the sea." Although Nebraska didn't appeal to him ("It's dull"), San Francisco did. "It's a very beautiful city, the east and the west together, very beautiful." But what struck him most was how little people knew or cared about the problems of his people. "They care about the latest song from Madonna, they care about their soccer games, their football, their wheat. But, except for a few people, nobody cares about the Middle East."

Radwan's trip infuriated the Israelis, who saw it as another opportunity for him to liaison with pro-PLO leaders. The Israelis point to meetings like those outside the territories, plus his endeavors inside the territories, as evidence of his dangerous work. They claim that he has actively supported the welfare of terrorist prisoners, including those responsible for the deaths of innocent Israelis; that he has organized a

teachers' association to strike against the Israeli government; and that he has helped to organize an overtly
anti-Israeli theater group, whose message is one of
violence. In 1987, after the deportation of Akram
Hania, editor of *A-Sha'ab* and now a personal assistant of Yasser Arafat, and after the imprisonment
of Faisal Husseini, who reportedly has close personal
ties to Arafat, a gap occurred in the PLO leadership
in the West Bank and Gaza. The Israelis say that
Radwan, considered to be next in the hierarchy,
stepped in to fill the void. His alleged assignments
included the channeling of money from Tunis and
Europe into the occupied territories; coordinating
with PLO efforts outside the territories; and activating
PLO uprisings, particularly from the Shabibah, inside
the West Bank and Gaza.

But so far the Israelis have not been able to suppress Radwan. Even his six months in prison are seen
as little more than a prolonged vacation in which he
strengthened his PLO connections and made important contacts with more radical elements, including
the Gaza-based Moslem fundamentalists. Says one official bitterly, "The PLO calls the Israeli jails 'schools
for the revolution financed by Israel.' " Indeed, unless
they deport him, the Israelis may not be able to punish
him more harshly because he is far too clever to carry
out any acts of violence himself. Another official compares Radwan Abu Ayash to Al Capone. "In the end,
you catch them on income tax, but you can never
catch them in the real thing. They always use third
parties to do things."

Although he will not speak openly about his work,
Radwan admits that he has supported many groups.
"I've done a lot of things," he says with a laugh. "It's
better to mention them collectively. I want my neck
to be all right."

His cool demeanor gives way to indignation as he
explains that many people still do not recognize that
the PLO has softened its stance. He is angry that

others refuse to think of the PLO as a potential peace-maker. "Nobody is hearing us. It's still that old image," he complains. The Palestinians, he says, have given up their old claims and their old ideas. "History is moving. You can't stick to the old theories. If the Israelis come and say they're ready to withdraw from the occupied territories of 1967, including east Jerusalem, and are ready to sign a peace treaty, we will do that now. We will go running after Arafat telling him to do this."

For many years, he says, if he had told his father to give up the dream of returning to Jaffa, his father would have been furious and would have considered the suggestion a betrayal. "If you heard someone talking about a Palestinian state only in the occupied territories, you would consider him a traitor. But today, we begin to think more reasonably and more pragmatically. We could not throw the Israelis into the sea, nor could the Israelis throw us into the desert; so we have to find a solution. Whether we like it or not, we have to learn to live with each other. Okay, we have a loaf of bread. Everybody claims that this loaf is his. But we'll have to share it. Nobody will starve if we share it."

Radwan says he will readily accept the notion of a separate state. "I don't mind it with open borders. I don't mind it with cooperation in all fields and demilitarization. Anything that might appeal to the Israelis, they can have. They can buy thirteen missiles from the United States and put them on the borders to guarantee their security; but we also want to guarantee our security."

Nevertheless, he finds it frustrating that the Israelis are not responding. The late Israeli defense minister Moshe Dayan once said, "I am waiting for a phone call from King Hussein." But now, says Radwan Abu Ayash, "The phone is ringing and ringing and ringing from the Palestinians, and nobody is picking it up."

THE CANDLES ARE BURNING

Now the distance is growing shorter
Today we are chanting a song for the coming days
A tragic song
After time has played on its strings
The songs of the widow
While it is not raining
Our thirsty hearts are resisting
All kinds of suffering
While spring has gone
And pains are full of grief
And sadness flows like water everywhere
Today we are scattering for the desert
The saga of the sad musical instrument
That is eager for the singer
We would like to say to history
Glorify the songs of challenge
That ignite for those lovers
The flame of the old beginnings.

　　　　—RADWAN ABU AYASH, from *Violin Melodies*

THE JEWISH FUNDAMENTALIST

Footsteps in the Bible

Miriam Levinger

*Miriam the prophetess . . . took a timbrel in her
hand; and all the women went out after her. . . .
And Miriam sang unto them:
Sing ye to the Lord, for He is highly exalted:
The horse and his rider hath He thrown into
the sea.*

—EXODUS 15:20

It takes forty-five minutes to make the drive from
Jerusalem to Hebron and almost as long to inch a car
through the crowded narrow streets of this bustling
Arab city. In this beleaguered period of the uprising,
the marketplace has been allowed open for only a few
hours every day, and thousands of Arab women, their
heads covered and their bodies draped in embroidered
cloth, now throng the shops and food stalls that spill
out from the sidewalks to the center of the square.
Long before sunrise, hundreds of Arab farmers trav-

eled here from miles around, their mules and horses
burdened with quantities of vegetables and fruits,
their open trucks carrying chickens, sheep, and goats
to slaughter in the wholesale market. The hot morning
air thickens with the putrid smell of slaughter and the
animal dung plopped in the streets and the stench
from the sewers that chokes one's breath. Screaming
sounds of Arabic assault the ear: farmers call across
the marketplace to one another, shouting above the
shrill voices of the women as they wrangle with the
vendors; the laughter and the shrieks of children min-
gle with the wail of the muezzin calling all the Moslems to prayer. Scattered everywhere are groups of
adolescents, restless from the endless months of closed
schools and no jobs, ever ready to throw some rocks
at an Israeli passerby.

In the midst of this cacophony walks Miriam Levinger, a Jewish woman from the Bronx, who has
scorned her classmates' comfortable dream of a split-
level house in Scarsdale and has raised her children
in the depths of this Arab stronghold. As she strolls
proudly through the square, shoulders thrown back,
arms thrust on her hips, her eyes stare straight ahead,
ignoring the Arabs who mob the streets, seeing only
the ancient stones where Abraham once trod and
where the patriarchs once prayed. She makes her way,
heedless of the danger, yet knowing full well that at
any moment, amid the crowds of Arab shoppers, a
terrorist may be lurking in a corner or hiding in the
myriad archways above the stalls, waiting to slip out
and slit her throat or stab her in the back.

Miriam Levinger is a figure of controversy, a hero
to some, a canister of hatred to others, well known
throughout Hebron and much of Israel for her daring,
defiant demonstrations of Jewish determination to establish a presence in the Arab city. She is Miriam, a
daughter of Abraham, sister of Aaron and Moses, a
woman whose calling it is to fulfill the words of the
Bible. When she and her husband came to Hebron

twenty years ago, they came because they received a
signal, a sign that they believe said, Go and settle this
land of the ancients. After the Arab-Israeli war in
1967, when the Jordanians lost the West Bank to the
Israelis, Miriam and Rabbi Levinger knew it was their
job to lead a handful of Jews and return to Hebron.
"The Six-Day War was of the Arabs' doing, so for
me it's a sign from God," she says. "All this land
where my forefathers trod came suddenly into our
possession again. My husband said, 'God did His; so
we have to do ours!' "

On this torrid June day, dressed simply in a short-
sleeve blue-and-white plaid blouse and brown pleated
skirt, with thick support stockings on her legs and
practical black rubber-soled shoes on her feet, she
walks alone, contemptuous of the crowds, daring the
Arabs to disturb her from her daily chores. She moves
slowly past shops that sell plastic dolls and cheap toys,
ignores the stalls where gold necklaces and earrings
are sold by their weight, glances at the big bins of
powdered spices—curry, cumin, oregano, and pep-
per—and looks purposefully at the open baskets of
fresh vegetables—plentiful supplies of potatoes, ripe
red tomatoes, yellow onions, white onions, several
varieties of lettuce, radishes, zucchini, and aubergines.
She stops for a moment and nods her kerchiefed head
toward a basket of onions. "How much?" she asks
the vendor in Hebrew. "Two shekels," he replies in
her language. She carefully chooses two dozen onions,
weighs them, and pays the old man his price. Now,
head held high, she walks briskly a few hundred feet
and stops before a small dark shop where the air inside
is dank with the heavy smell of sesame and olive oils.
Again she asks how much, and the seller answers her
in Arabic. "Ten shekels." "Are you kidding?" she says
brazenly in pidgin Arabic. "Last week it was eight
shekels." The man turns to his boss, who shrugs his
shoulders and nods in concession. In the style of generations past, he presses out a liter of thick golden

oil. Satisfied, Miriam pays him the money. "It isn't the two shekels I care about," she says later. "But if I let him get away with it, then next week it will be twelve shekels and the week after, fourteen. After all, this is the Middle East."

Miriam Levinger came to the Middle East an idealistic eighteen-year-old, who had left New York against the wishes of her parents and set off on Passover to make *aliyah*, uncertain where God would lead her. Now, nearly thirty years later, her supporters call her a seer. "She is the spirit of Israel," says Israel Harel, one of the leaders of the settlers' movement. "She has set the way for many people."

In the spring of 1968, ten months after the Six-Day War, she and her Israeli-born husband, Moshe, a rabbi, came to Hebron. Their professed reason was to celebrate the eight days of Passover, the holiday that recalls the Jewish exodus from slavery in Egypt. In reality, they were determined to claim the ancient lands of Judea and Samaria. Tricking the Israeli government, whose policy at the time was not to let Jews move into Arab cities and to allow the Arabs to lead their normal lives, the Levingers told the military governor that they wanted to spend Passover in Hebron, and took rooms at a hotel near the dusty entrance to the town. But after the holiday was over, the Levingers refused to leave. They yearned to be near the burial site of Abraham and his wife, Sarah; of Isaac and Rebecca; Jacob and Leah. Their goal was to settle in Hebron, this holy place where Jews had lived from the days of Abraham until the destruction of the Temple. Even afterward, small groups of Jews had lived there until the Arabs massacred sixty-seven of them in 1929 and the rest were forced to leave.

Seventy thousand Israelis have followed in the Levingers' footsteps, settling the sweeping hilltops of Judea and Samaria, boldly building their starkly modern compounds that look down so brazenly upon the old and crudely built Arab towns. For each of them

Miriam Levinger is a model of the Jewish matriarch, a proud, persistent, pious woman, who rears her children in the spirit of Sarah and Rebecca and risks her life so that the Jews may live in the biblical Eretz Yisrael.

But the Arabs who have been living here were not so easily convinced nor so ready to give up their farms and their homes. Miriam Levinger's Jewish detractors—and they are many—believe that she has carried the word of God too far, defying the government of Israel and jeopardizing the lives of her countrymen. Since the days when the Levingers first arrived in Hebron, the town has become a microcosm of the conflict between the Palestinians and the Israelis: hundreds of Arabs and dozens of Jews have been killed; the Levingers' son-in-law has been imprisoned for life; Israeli politics have been torn asunder; and the very soul of Israel has come under question.

Around the corner from the teeming market is a small square where the mood is quieter and the air is still. Here a stone plaque marks the place where Aaron Gross, a nineteen-year-old talmudic student, was murdered and chopped up by four Arab boys several years ago. A few feet away, an enclave of white stone houses rises out of the earth, buildings so at one with the land that they look both ancient and modern, cavelike and contemporary. Israeli soldiers, wearing olive-green uniforms and carrying walkie-talkies and machine guns, stand on guard, some on the rooftops, some on the ground, placed there ostensibly to protect the few dozen Israeli families who live here from the Arabs. But some would argue that the defense force is present just as much to protect the Arabs from the Jews.

Above the soldiers is the old Jewish quarter of Hebron, where a dozen old houses cluster around the sixteenth-century Avraham Avinu synagogue. A flight of winding stone stairs leads up to the figure of a woman highlighted in the brilliant sunshine. Miriam Levinger stands proudly in front of her door, her hand resting near the mezuzah that proclaims this a Jewish home. In the tradition of orthodox women, her head is covered, a brown cloth pinned to her graying brown hair. She uses no cosmetics. A thin gold necklace and a plain gold wedding band are her only adornments.

She welcomes her visitors and brings them inside the thick stone house with its curved walls and arched ceilings that date from four hundred years ago; now she and her family rent their sparsely furnished home from the Israeli government. Up a few stone steps and to the right is the square kitchen, where a barely adequate refrigerator and small stove take care of the family's needs; although it is still early in the day, the smells of Shabbat dinner float through the air. A few more steps lead to the bedrooms where Miriam and her husband and the youngest five of their eleven children sleep. In the days when the Jordanians occupied this town, they razed the community's Avraham Avinu synagogue and used this house as a goat pen. Miriam laughs now as she refers to her children's dormitory as the "kids' room." She guides her guests to the living room with its cool tile floors and walls lined with leather-bound books, nods toward the sofa, covered casually with a gray jacquard cloth, and settles herself in a hard wooden chair.

"Do you mind if I smoke?" she asks in an accent that still smacks of New York, and lights a Montana, an Israeli cigarette. She draws in on the tobacco, admonishes herself because smoking is considered inappropriate for religious women, and compares her precarious existence now with what it was. "Life is easier here than in the east Bronx," she laughs. Her clear brown eyes smile from a face that has few lines, kept smooth perhaps by the purity of her vision. When she speaks seriously, her eyes have a distant, almost mystical gaze as though she were looking back into the past as well as into the future. At fifty years old, she is secure in her knowledge of who she is and why she is here.

"I am part of the Jewish people and I must do individually what the Jewish people as a whole has to do," she says. "Because of that I am sitting here in Hebron."

Hebron, the land of the patriarchs where Abraham paid four hundred shekels for a burial place for his wife, Sarah; Hebron, the land that David ruled for seven years before he went to Jerusalem; Hebron, sister city to Jerusalem and the second-holiest city for Jews. Miriam Levinger feels it is only natural that the Jews should be here now. To her, Hebron represents the beginnings, the place where the Jews grew as a biblical nation, and the place where they must grow again. She is a child of the Bible and believes that its message states clearly that Israel is the land of the Jews, the land where the Jews belong, and the land that they must serve.

"There are certain main themes in Jewish history," she says emphatically, "written down in black on white." She is a daughter of the Diaspora, a woman driven by the words *Next year in Jerusalem* and by the principle of Eretz Yisrael. Over and over she repeats the words of the Bible, "Israel I gave to you, I gave to Abraham, to Isaac and Jacob, Israel I gave to you." She takes her lessons from the rabbis of the Talmud, the prophets who begged the Jews to return from their exile in Babylon. She speaks of the wise men who blamed the Jews themselves for the destruction of the Second Temple in A.D. 70 because the Jewish people, content with life in Babylon, refused to return to Israel to rebuild their land. Miriam quotes Santayana ("If you don't learn from history, then you will be forced to relive it") and Barbara Tuchman ("She says there aren't really any reasons for anti-Semitism; there are always excuses"). She talks of the Holocaust, and of the blindness of the Jews in all of Europe—particularly in Germany, from which her husband's family fled, and in Hungary, from which her own grandparents could not. She tells about her cousin who now lives in Tel Aviv, but who more than forty years ago was an inmate in Auschwitz. There in the concentration camp, she watched as her mother, her sister, and her grandmother were led to the ovens and burned. Now Levinger says she takes it very seriously when Arab leaders say they want to destroy the Jews.

Miriam Levinger sees the future strength of Israel in the lessons of its past. "For the Jewish people to come into their own, after two thousand years of Diaspora, they have to start all over again," she says. "That begins from the tie to Israel." All Jews, she insists, "whether they are orthodox, reform, or secular, must recognize absolutely that there is only one place in the world to which they truly belong—and that is Israel."

At three A.M. on a cold April night during Passover, 1979, Miriam Levinger roused her seven small children from their sleep. Pulling them from their beds against their will, she squeezed their bare feet into their socks and shoes and buttoned up their coats over their pajamas. Over and over the children cried and complained and tried to climb back into their beds, but Miriam would not be stopped. Listening to her children's protests, she fought off fears that maybe she was crazy and told herself to remember the words of Rabbi Nachman of Breslau: "When a person wants to do a good deed, all the objections in the world suddenly rise up before his eyes." Several times she reminded herself of these words and fought off her own impulse to quit. Then, as the last child was buttoned up and ready to go, all of the children seemed to come alive and fall into the spirit of the plan. And at that moment, Miriam knew that the rabbi's spirit was with her and what she was doing was right.

When they had arrived in Hebron in 1968, the

Levingers and their followers had gained a concession from the government and for the first two years were permitted to live as squatters inside the compound of the military governor. They continued their struggle, and in 1970 a compromise was reached: the Levingers were granted the right to live not inside but outside the city. They were given homes and land to settle in an area called Kiryat Arba. But after several years Miriam Levinger was still frustrated in her dream to penetrate the town. From the beginning she had told her husband, the spiritual leader of the settlement, that she wanted to establish a foothold smack in the center of the city. Now was the time to do it.

The Levingers conspired with several other couples, all of whom lived at Kiryat Arba, their compound in the hills above Hebron. Together the men had come up with a plan to take over a building once used by the army but now abandoned, save for a few Arab shops in the rear. The building, known as Beit Hadassah, had been established as a Jewish clinic, one of the first Hadassah projects completed at the beginning of the twentieth century. It was the site where the family of a Jewish pharmacist named Gershon was brutally murdered, the first victims of the Arab massacre in 1929. Now, by this very act of reclaiming the building, the settlers would begin to avenge the death of the Jews and, says Levinger, to "wipe out the shame of 1929."

Knowing that the government was against the idea of Israelis provoking the Arabs by living in their town, the settlers plotted to make their move under cover of darkness. They sent the women and children first so that the Israeli soldiers would neither attack them nor try to eject them from the house. With their thirty little ones bundled up, the twenty women, some of them pregnant, climbed onto the settlement's truck and lay down on the floor, hiding from the Israeli soldier on duty at the gate. They drove the few miles down the road to Hebron and steered the truck to the large stone building that once served as both a clinic and a school. From the truck they took a long ladder and leaned it against the building's walls. Slowly the women and children climbed up the ladder and, through a broken window, entered the house. To keep their offspring warm during the night, the women fed them oranges and matzos, and by daybreak the children started to sing. When the soldiers finally found them and asked how they had arrived, the youngsters told them they had been led there by Abraham, Isaac, and Jacob.

For more than a year some of the families lived in the house. At first the Israeli soldiers would not permit them to leave and reenter, and for six months they lived without water, electricity, or men. But after a while life became more normal, until January 1980, when Yoshua Saloma, a yeshiva student walking in the marketplace, was stabbed to death by an Arab. Saloma's murder became a rallying cry for the settlers. "Your death will be a service to our cause," Rabbi Meir Kahane, leader of the fanatical Kach movement, announced to Saloma's mourners, and the cycle of violence had begun.

After much debate in the Knesset, the government finally decided to give the settlers three locations inside Hebron: Beit Hadassah could be used as a yeshiva and home for several families; the decaying handful of houses and the synagogue in the Jewish quarter would be turned over to them; and the tombs of the patriarchs would be open to them for private worship at designated times.

The Arabs, finding the decision offensive, reacted in a panic and the mood turned black. The mayor of Hebron, Fahd Kawassme, organized mass gatherings and militant demonstrations in the streets. On the evening of May 1, a group of *cheder* yeshiva students on their way from synagogue to Beit Hadassah were attacked and shot by Arab terrorists. Six of the students, who were combining their studies with military duty, were instantly killed and several others badly wounded. Later that night the mayor of Hebron, the grand mufti of Hebron, and the mayor of neighboring Halhul were all deported.

Those who know the story from the Arab side tell it somewhat differently. Darwish Nasser, the Palestinian lawyer for the attackers, claims that the house called Beit Hadassah was not abandoned at all, but had been occupied by Arabs since 1929. "Arabs lived in the house," he says. "The women came and occupied the house and after that they threw the Arabs out." Adds Nasser, "Many, many ministers and officials condemned this step by the settlers." As he recalls the incident, the yeshiva students, who Miriam Levinger acknowledges were soldiers as well as students, had come from Kiryat Arba to pray at the tomb of the patriarchs. After prayers, says Nasser, the soldier-students "passed by Beit Hadassah to encourage the women and were singing and dancing in the streets." So, in what he admits was "a well-planned assassination . . . they were attacked by four Palestinians. Six were killed and about eighteen were injured."

The death of the students brought a terrible burden of guilt on Miriam Levinger. Without her activities, everyone knew, the boys would not have been there; the heat of their mothers' anger burned through her. "After they were killed, I had to do a lot of thinking," she confesses. "I imagine that in their parents' hearts they felt that if perhaps their sons weren't in Hebron, then it wouldn't have happened." But then again, she says, "Being a Jew and being in Israel, if you're not attacked here, then you're attacked there. And if you're not attacked in Israel, then you're attacked in Brussels or in Istanbul." Even as she speaks, the squawking sounds of a walkie-talkie can be heard coming from her kitchen, a reminder that she and her neighbors live in constant fear of attack. From the little black box, she is always in communication with

Hebronites in the settlements, in the local yeshivas, and in their cars, ready to reach for their guns and call in the army should a problem arise.

After the murder of the yeshiva students, the settlers raged with anger, furious not only at the Arabs but at the Israeli government and the army for not fully protecting them. Several years earlier, in 1974, in the aftermath of the Yom Kippur War and the first Israeli disengagement from the Sinai, some Israelis, including Rabbi Levinger, felt bitter about the withdrawal. In response, they had formed a group called Gush Emunim ("Bloc of the Faithful"), a fundamentalist religious organization whose purpose was to pursue with a vengeance the establishment of Israeli towns and villages in the occupied territories. After the Camp David Accords in 1978, members of the Gush Emunim felt its efforts had been thwarted and that they had been betrayed by the Begin government because it was willing to make peace with Egypt and to compromise the plan for settlement expansion. The Gush formed an underground group, which then masterminded a plot to destroy the holiest Moslem site in Jerusalem, the Dome of the Rock. Over the course of several years they developed a plan for twenty-four Israeli terrorists to use a mass of precision bombs, guns, and gas to blow up the mosque, leaving the surrounding site undamaged.

It was during the planning stages of this event that the yeshiva students were killed on their way to Beit Hadassah. The Gush Emunim members felt that the government had let them down and even abetted the Arab murderers, whom they believed to be members of a front organization for the PLO called the Palestinian National Guidance Committee. The committee of twenty-one members had been formed in order to stop any Palestinian segment from accepting the Camp David Accords. The very fact that the Israeli government allowed the committee to exist was seen by the Gush Emunim as a kind of complicity.

Three members of the Gush, young men who had grown up with the Levingers and had been nursed on the blood of Hebron and raised on the fodder of fanaticism, decided to take matters into their own hands. After two meetings in their homes, which were also attended by the rabbis, they drew up a scheme to bomb the cars of three Arab mayors, all of whom were active in the Palestinian National Guidance Committee. Their plan was not to kill the mayors, but to maim them, creating crippled symbols of Israeli revenge. In fact, two of the mayors lost their legs; the third escaped unharmed.

Over the course of the next few years tensions mounted and the air became more charged. Miriam Levinger recalls, "The situation was very, very tense. In Hebron the atmosphere was just like before a pogrom." This time, in broad daylight, a yeshiva student named Aaron Gross was murdered, his body chopped into pieces and left just outside the marketplace. At first the boy was mistaken for an Arab, and when Miriam Levinger, who had been trained as a nurse, was asked to help the bleeding victim, she refused.

The Gush Emunim group would not allow this murder to go unavenged. In July 1983 the same three fanatical Hebronites approached the Islamic college in Hebron and, just as classes were ending at lunchtime, threw hand grenades and fired guns at the students, killing three people and wounding thirty-three others.

As the violence continued, Arab terrorists killed more Israelis, and the Gush planned its last act of revenge. In 1984, with the endorsement of Hebron rabbis and almost certainly, though it remains unproven, with a nod from Moshe Levinger, the group plotted to blow up five buses filled with Arab passengers. Once again they meticulously laid out every detail of the action and carefully wired the buses under their fuel tanks so that the explosions would be devastating. But the Israeli secret police had discovered their activities, and moments after the wiring, the group were arrested. Later, when they were put on trial, the plot to destroy the Dome of the Rock was revealed. Three of the Jewish terrorists were sentenced to life imprisonment: one of them, Shaul Nir, lived next door to the Levingers and had helped to build their house; another, Menahamen Levni, had worked closely with Moshe Levinger and was in charge of developing the Jewish section of Hebron; the third was Uzi Sharbaf, the son-in-law of Moshe and Miriam Levinger.

"I had to think it out," she says now, as the wail of the muezzin in the background calls Moslems to noontime prayers. "What I think is that the government has to be firm and do what it should in order to protect the lives of the citizens." To her the Israeli government had not been firm enough with the Arabs and had not recognized their real intent. "We have to realize that what the Arabs write and what they proclaim and what they say, they really mean. If they have the Palestinian charter, that means they want to erase Israel physically and kill the Jews."

Miriam Levinger was born in Brooklyn and moved to the Bronx when she was five. Her parents had come to America in 1927, and for many of the Jews who escaped the persecutions in the ghettos of Germany and the pogroms in the *shtetls* of Eastern Europe, the Bronx was paradise. Home was in one of the dozens of apartment houses that lined the Grand Concourse or in the brownstones and tenements along the side streets. Jobs were readily available, just a subway ride away in Manhattan or, in the case of Miriam's father, in a nearby synagogue, where he was a cantor. Little Miriam lived with her family on Southern Boulevard and 163d Street and went to PS 75, only a few blocks away. But it wasn't recollections of the classroom that so vividly stayed with her. "I grew up with this memory of World War Two," she says, "my mother sitting by the window and crying. It's a childhood memory that forever goes with me. I'll never forget it when the people came to tell her how her parents were taken to Auschwitz and how they were killed." Miriam's eyes fill with tears and her voice tightens as she says, "Eighty percent of my family went up the chimney, and I grew up with that. That is what makes me tick. I am fulfilling a mission for all those who died." With those words the sound of revenge fills the air. Silently, perhaps even unconsciously, she sends a message that the Arabs who dare to live here will pay the price for the Jews who have died.

Miriam was a good student and her teachers recommended she attend Hunter High School in Manhattan, where students were screened and only the brighter ones were accepted. At Hunter the world unfolded, exposing her to a life that reached way beyond the ghettos of the Bronx. Like so many children of immigrant families, the girls she knew were anxious to be accepted into this new culture, eager to cast aside the weight of their Jewish past and to be assimilated into American society. Says Miriam, "They had an identity crisis. They didn't know if they were coming or going." But she had no such problem. "I had my priorities. I took my Jewish background seriously."

In addition to her high school classes, Miriam attended the Teachers Institute, where she took courses in the evening. With great fear, she would take the subway home from school every night, scared of the drunks and the weirdos who rode with her on the train. When she got off at her stop, her walk home was an obstacle course. "We had two bars on our street, and you always had drunks roaming the sidewalks and the gutters," she recalls. "I always had the feeling that any cuckoo would come along and kill me."

Now, she says, all you have to do is open a *New York Post* to see how many people are pointlessly murdered there every day. "For what sake do the Jews who live in New York risk their lives? For the sake of the Diaspora?" she asks, shrugging her shoulders and throwing her hands up in despair. She readily admits that here in Hebron her life is also in danger. But here, she says, she is risking her life for a higher purpose, "for the sake of rebuilding Israel, so my situation is better than theirs." In New York, she adds, "there is no rhyme or reason. Here in Hebron there are terrorists and two groups of people who believe they are right. So if there is murder here, at least it has rhyme and reason."

She feels protected too by her own people, by the Israeli soldiers who guard the area night and day, by the fact that she has her own government, and because "I don't have to exist on the goodwill of others." How different, she says, from the helplessness of New York or, worse, from the pogroms of Russia, the Holocaust of the Nazis, or further back, from the slaughter of the Inquisition. "I don't have to go like a ram to slaughter. I have my own Israeli troops to defend me."

Miriam Levinger says she is comfortable in this city of Moslem fundamentalists, comfortable in the streets, comfortable in the shops, comfortable with the people. "It's a very honest relationship," she says, "much more honest than I had in America. We both know where the other stands." Although the dialogue in Hebron between the Jews and Arabs is most often correct and to the point, once in a while there is room for a smile. The opponents even look to each other for answers to their seemingly insoluble problems. Not long ago, when her husband went to the Israeli bank where he does business, one of the Arab tellers stopped him. "How long till there will be peace, Rabbi?" the teller asked. "It will take at least one hundred years," Levinger replied. The Arab was taken aback: "You mean, I won't live to see it, and not even

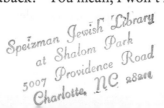

my son will live to see it?" Levinger laughed, and
feeling generous he replied, "For you, fifty years."

The interaction here between the Jews and the
Arabs is basically mercantile: the Jews need the Arabs
for their goods and services, and the Arabs need the
Jews for their business. But more than that, in some
ways they have learned to live with one another, to
understand each other's faith, even to speak each other's words.

Miriam is careful not to let the understandings
move too far, and she keeps her conversations to a
minimum. She has no Arab friends, and when she was
invited to an Arab home, she refused. "I'll be very
frank with you," she says. "The reason I don't encourage too close a relationship is because I saw in
America that close relationships lead to assimilation."
Besides, she adds, "The Arabs in Hebron, they also
wouldn't like seeing intermarriages, and we don't
like seeing intermarriages."

In this Moslem city where religion is as funda-
mental as food and water, where there are no hotels,
and where movie theaters, liquor stores, and even a
drop of beer is forbidden, no one begrudges another's
religious needs. "They respect religion," Miriam explains. "They're religious in Hebron and we're religious also. So on that we understand each other very
well. When it comes to young girls or attitudes toward
women, we understand each other very well."

They know each others' holidays and even respect
the smaller rituals. They know the name of each
special day, what it is for, and how it is celebrated.
Just before one Purim, an early spring celebration
when children dress up like kings and queens and use
noisemakers to scare off the ancient Haman, (evil ad-
viser to the Persian king Ahasuerus) Miriam went to
a local Arab shop to buy some makeup. When she
asked for the cosmetics, the sales clerk showed her
some high-priced products. But the owner quickly re-

alized that she needed the makeup for her children. "It's for *id el mashara*," he knowingly told the clerk, using the Arab name for Purim. "Their holiday is coming. Show her something cheap. She needs it for her daughters."

Routine chores, like going to the drugstore or shopping for food, fill her days. "I have five children at home," she explains. "I have laundry, and I have to cook, and I have to shop, and I have to clean. I'm busy the whole day just with housework."

But there are also moments of sheer joy, times spent once a week with a dozen or so other women who gather at the tombs of the patriarchs. There, in the center of Hebron, vestiges of earlier occupations still stand. On top of the steps and rounded stone walls built under the Roman King Herod, a large mosque stands from the seventh century A.D. Inside the Islamic building that encases the tombs, mosaic patterns decorate the stone floors, stained-glass panels grace the windows, and intricate paintings in blue and gold cover the ceilings. Elaborate pillars and minarets protect each tomb and set it off for the worshipers. On Fridays the mosque is open only to Moslems; at sundown, only the Jews are allowed to pray. Most of the time the system works, but the tension lately has been electric and fights have broken out.

Those who work here know that every Monday morning a group of Jewish women from Hebron come and set a circle of wooden folding chairs next to the tomb of Abraham and Sarah. Most of the women are young mothers in their twenties and thirties, dressed in skirts and blouses with large kerchiefs on their heads. Two of the women are Miriam's daughters; one is the wife of Uzi Sharbaf, the terrorist in prison. They come with their diapered infants in strollers, their older babies toddling along. On this June morning, the children wander around the circle, sometimes playing with their Fisher Price telephones and rattles, other times sharing their bottles and their teething

rings. Across the hall from the women, three or four
Moslems kneel on the ground and pray. The women,
led by Miriam Levinger, take turns reading aloud the
psalms of David, Solomon, and Asaph and then say
the ancient prayers by themselves. All of the group
quietly say special prayers for women who are child-
less, for those who are sick, and for those who should
marry. When one woman shed tears with her prayers,
Miriam looked at her said, "She had something on
her heart. She's crying bitterly to her mother, Sarah."

For Miriam the thousands of years since the days
of Abraham have almost disappeared. "For us," she
says, "four thousand years is like yesterday." She has
skipped the space between generations and shortened
the umbilical cord. She lives in the time of the Bible,
walks in the steps of the patriarchs, and speaks to her
ancestors as though they were her parents and she is
their child. "With our forefathers the relationship is
direct," she says. "We feel toward them as if we are
their first children. And they feel toward us as if we
are their first children."

Miriam's own children, raised to walk alone
among the Arabs, are imbued with that same sense
of history, that same closeness to their kin. When her
oldest son, Ephraim, named for her grandfather who
died in the Holocaust, reached the age of thirteen and
was ready for his bar mitzvah, there was no question
of where the ceremony would be. It took place in the
courtyard of the cave of the Machpelah. Because of
that, she says, her children continue their biblical lin-
eage, even softening in their way some of the horror
of the concentration camps and the Holocaust. "The
victims didn't die, do you understand? Because we are
continuing them, continuing them better than where
they were."

The questions of Who am I?, the searches for one's
roots, the doubts of the Diaspora have no part in her
children's lives. "They have a very strong sense of
identity." she says. "I have highly motivated children

who know why they were born and what they are
alive for."

Miriam Levinger knows why she was born and
where she will die. "I'm very happy to be part of this
generation where the return has begun, the reawak-
ening and the stirring as a Jew in my own land," she
says. "All over the world, Jewish communities started
with a few families coming in—look at Frankfurt or
Baghdad—and the Jews settled down and eventually
the population grew until it became a great Jewish
community. This happened all over the world
throughout history, and it can happen in Israel also.
I think that eventually it's an evolutionary process;
as time goes on, if the Jews are secure in themselves
and secure in their sovereignty over Eretz Yisrael, then
the Arabs themselves will receive the idea of Jewish
sovereignty. And those who don't, well, they have
somewhere to go. Those Arabs who accept the situation will remain, and those who don't accept it,
won't." As for the possibility of giving up Judea and
Samaria, she adds, "I don't contemplate it, because I
believe in truth." For the Arabs who live there, the
truth may look a little different. But for Miriam Levinger, the truth is in the past, and the past is in the
future.

THE GAZA STRIP

Breeding Ground for the Intifada

Haidar Abdul Shafi

"At noon on Sunday, December 6, 1987, Israeli plastics salesman Shlomo Sakal was removing merchandise from his truck on the main street of Gaza when he was stabbed to death. Two days later, on Tuesday afternoon, an Israeli truck smashed into a car carrying Arab workers home from work in Israel. Four Arabs were killed; others were wounded. That same evening, hundreds of bitter and resentful people gathered in a few locations, particularly in Jabalya refugee camp, the largest camp in Gaza. The demonstrators claimed that the accident was deliberate and that the Israeli driver did it as a vendetta. The next morning, December 9, hundreds of students gathered in school-yards, organized a strong protest, and threw stones at Israeli patrols. Similar demonstrations erupted in other parts of Gaza. That evening an Israeli military spokesman announced that three Arab

youths had been killed and twenty wounded. In
the painful chronicle of the Arab-Israeli conflict,
those events marked the beginning of the popular
uprising known as the intifada."
——DANNY RUBINSTEIN, *Davar*

Only five miles wide and twenty-five miles long, Gaza
can hardly contain the refugees, much less their anger.
Their passions have erupted in almost continuous violence since Israel conquered the narrow strip of land
more than two decades ago. Here, generations sprout
on top of one another because there is no other space
for expansion.

Ask any teenager in Jabalya where he is from, and
he will not tell you Block C or Jabalya. He will tell you
he is from Kharatia, even though he has never seen it.
The camps have accomplished a purpose: maintaining
the mental presence of the homeland and keeping to
the old village structures. The families from a particular village or town still live together; marriages are arranged beween their sons and daughters; and even the
old hierarchy is still in place: the elderly Arab who was
the *mukhtar*, the traditional religious leader, of Kharatia continues to be the *mukhtar* of Block C. It is all
intended, of course, to keep the memory alive.

This is a world where poverty and privilege clash,
a breeding ground for bitterness and anger that has
spawned a new legion of young Islamic fundamentalists. Their adamant rejection of any compromise
with Israel and their willingness to sacrifice their own
lives have jolted them to the forefront of the struggle.
It is these fresh-faced teenagers, members of the shad-
owy forces of the Islamic Jihad, who have inherited
the mantle that belonged to Fatah, the mainstream
PLO group whose early recruits also came from the
slums of Gaza.

In the thirty years since Fatah was first begun, the
population of the camps has doubled to over 350,000.
Little else has changed in the squalid camps: in spite

of the huge mounds of garbage overflowing the trash cans, you can still read the red-painted UNRWA acronyms on the rusted oil barrels; there is still the awful stench from the open sewers and the constant buzzing of flies; and unaware of it all, small children still play on the wide dirt alley that is the camp's main boulevard. Once in a while a vendor arrives from outside, pushing his gypsy-painted wooden cart past the high concrete walls, selling emaciated versions of sugar-coated candy apples.

Today, Gaza is a combat zone. Large parts of Gaza City are under curfew; barbed wire is rolled across the streets. Israeli soldiers stand near the barriers, and clusters of troops patrol the deserted streets, their tear gas canisters and machine guns ready to be used whenever someone threatens the uneasy truce.

Amid the filth and the stench, the outbreaks of cholera and the uprisings of anger, Haidar Abdul Shafi provides the Gazans with a glimmer of hope. While the masses suffer the deathly illnesses caused by over-spilling cesspools and noxious air, he rules the Red Crescent, overseeing the clinics and the ambulances that often save their lives. But more than that, he speaks for their dreams, representing them at the highest political levels, fighting continuously for their right to self-determination. He is the premier pro-PLO champion in Gaza for Palestinian nationalism. Tall and stout, stern-faced and stalwart, his patrician background and aristocratic air are in sharp contrast to the pathetic prostration of Gaza's refugees. He lives in a rarified world; an American-educated surgeon who speaks with an upper-class accent, he supported the ideas of Gamal Abdel Nasser, tried to snuff the hopes of Anwar Sadat, and snubbed his nose at Moshe Dayan. He is urbane and highly intelligent, proudly defiant and fiercely independent, a man who suffers Israeli occupation by stubbornly refusing to give in.

In the teeming center of Gaza City, minutes away from the swarming streets of the camps, a tiny oasis

of civility exists behind an iron gate. From the entry-
way to his house in the heart of town, sixty-three-
year-old Haidar welcomes guests to his fortified villa,
a one-story stone residence hidden by walls, protected
by bars on the windows and a security system, em-
braced by palm trees and flowering bushes. With a
polite smile and a powerful handshake, he ushers his
visitors into the living room and, like a French no-
bleman, offers a seat on the Louis XV-style furniture.
Embroidered floral cushions grace the sofas, European landscape paintings dot the walls, and precious
Persian rugs warm the floors. His wife, Hoda, scion
of a prominent Palestinian family, offers Turkish coffee in china cups. They speak of their children who
study abroad, of their own luxurious days in Alexandria, and of their privileged youth. Yet beneath the
polished manners and civilized demeanor lie anger
and frustration as great as any refugee's. For Haidar
Abdul Shafi feels betrayed, betrayed by the Arabs who
took away his homeland, betrayed by the Egyptians
who lost his land to Israel, betrayed by the Palestinians
who tried to destroy him. But most of all he feels
betrayed by the Jews, by the Jews who once needed
him and now rule him, by the Jews who turned his
vision of independence into a state of their own.

Sheikh Muhyidin was a rich and powerful man in the
part of the British mandate called Gaza. As head of
the Waqf, (the Moslem religions endowment), he was
custodian of all the Islamic property. His duties were
to oversee the enormous amounts of land and estates
left to the Moslem foundation; to distribute them to
the poor; use them for religious support, educational
institutions, or welfare purposes; and to invest them
for future growth. Not only was he important to the
poor because he could disburse the income, but also
to the wealthy because he could help them avoid tax-
ation and appropriation by donating their land to the
Waqf.

In 1925, when his son Haidar was four years old, the sheikh and his family were transferred to Hebron, burial place of the patriarchs, and holy ground for Moslems as well as Jews. In Hebron, a small community of Jews lived side by side with the Arab majority, sometimes even living in the same apartment houses.

Across the hall from the Shafis lived a religious Jewish family. Early each Saturday morning there would be a knock on the Shafis' door. Could little Haidar please come over? With great pride, the boy would enter the apartment and do the task that the orthodox Jews were not permitted to do, snuffing out the Sabbath candles.

Once in a while another Jew would come to call; the chief rabbi of Hebron would visit Haidar's father to discuss any problems that may have occurred at the holy site. There, at the tombs of Abraham and Sarah, both religious groups prayed, but the Jews were permitted to reach only the seventh step of the shrine. Since the twelfth century the monument, built earlier by Herod, had been declared off-limits to the Jews. Even standing outside had to be approved by the Arab sheikh. "My father had a great deal of tolerance toward Judaism," Haidar recalls.

For two years, he saw little else of the Jews, and in 1927 his family returned to Gaza, where there were almost no Jews at all. When the boy was ten, news of the terrible massacre of sixty-seven Jews in Hebron reached Gaza. "Most of us deplored what had happened," he says. Nevertheless, he faults the Jews, blaming their murders on the spread of "Zionist propaganda," aimed at "uprooting the Palestinian people."

But Haidar had other concerns. His education in Gaza was stymied by the lack of secondary schools— the fifty thousand Arabs who lived there were mostly farmers and had no need for higher education. As a young adolescent he was sent to Jerusalem to study

at the Arab College. But his stay was cut short when
riots and a six-month strike against the British forced
the closing of his school.

In 1937 he went off to Lebanon to be educated
at the American University of Beirut, where, he says,
"one of my best friends was a Jew." Emmanuel Margoliash had come from Egypt and, like Haidar, was
studying medicine. The two classmates were "intimate
friends," says Haidar, and their contacts lasted until
the 1950s. Years later, Haidar tried to reach Margoliash, but his efforts were to no avail.

While he was at the university, Haidar joined the
Arab Nationalist Movement, an organization that attracted upper-class university students interested in
promoting Arab nationalism and a Palestinian state.
Since the university was against any student political
involvement, "we had primarily cultural activities,"
says Haidar, "oriented in a nationalist sense." But he
also notes that much of their attention was focused
on dealing with the "Zionist program." He could accept the religious beliefs of his friend Margoliash, but
not the Jewish nationalism that many were promoting.

After graduation, Haidar returned to Palestine,
and despite his pro-Arab nationalism, he joined the
British army, expecting to fight against the Nazis on
the western front. But his batallion, kept in an army
camp in Gaza, never saw action, and in 1945 he returned to civilian life. But if he had missed the agony
of one war, in the next few years he would see his
share of armed struggle and more.

In May 1948, as the Jews prepared to declare their
independent state and the Arabs were readying to fight
the United Nations partition plan, skirmishes began
along the coastline. As the combat continued, cities
and villages were disrupted, and tens of thousands of
people fled their homes. Within several months two
hundred thousand Arabs from Haifa, Jaffa, and other
towns had flooded into Gaza seeking refuge from the

war. Instead of shelter, those who came to Gaza found a tiny strip of land, filled with makeshift camps, muddy paths, and putrid air. Their meals were little more than milk and flour; their homes were nothing more than canvas tents. As a doctor, Haidar could try to minister to their wounds, but he could not help the wretchedness of poverty or the pain of homelessness.

A year later he left; he could not do much for the future of the refugees, but at least he could further his own career. He spent the next four years in the United States, studying surgery at the Miami Valley Hospital in Dayton, Ohio. Like so many other privileged Palestinians, he thought about staying to earn his fortune, but family ties and a deep feeling for his homeland brought him back to Gaza.

When Haidar returned in 1954 to the swarming Gaza Strip, he saw at once that major changes had been made. Although, unlike Jordan and the West Bank, the Egyptians had not annexed Gaza nor given its residents passports, they had greatly improved the educational system, establishing many schools and requiring compulsory attendance for every child over the age of six. In addition, the Egyptians had opened their own universities to secondary-school graduates, offering college education without the cost of tuition. Every year at least two thousand Palestinians could attend the universities. The rural society that had lost its land could now benefit from a more sophisticated civilization; their sons would be doctors, lawyers, engineers, and pharmacists who could work throughout the Arab world.

Nevertheless, the squalid conditions in Gaza served as a breeding ground for guerrillas. Those who did not go to university could join the Palestinian *fedayeen* and, carrying weapons from Egypt into Gaza, use the Strip as their base of operations for commando raids into Israel. The leader of these guerrillas was Ahmed Shukeiry. Yasser Arafat also was in

Gaza, organizing Palestinian students; the following
year he would become a leader in Fatah, the most
important militant nationalist group.

Haidar was impressed by the Egyptian support
for the Palestinians and went to work for the Egyptians, serving as a surgeon in Tal Zahur Hospital. Two
years later on a trip to the Egyptian port of Alexandria, his friends introduced him to Hoda Khalidi, a
nineteen-year-old girl from a prominent Jerusalem
family that had fled to Egypt after the Arab-Israeli
war. Haidar was thirty-eight and eager to start a family; the couple agreed to marry.

But their plans were disrupted when the Israelis
invaded Egypt and occupied Gaza in the process. "It
was a completely hostile relationship between the Israelis and the Palestinians." At the hospital where he
had volunteered, three shells hit the grounds and two
nurses were fatally wounded. "They were very brutal.
I think many people were killed unnecessarily," Haidar says bitterly. Dozens of Arabs were detained,
among them one of Haidar's patients, who disappeared. Despite protests to the Red Cross and to the
UN, the Israelis gave no information on what had
happened to the detainees. "Then one day," Haidar
recalls, "there were heavy rains in Gaza, and the rushing water in the outskirts of the city removed some
of the soil. Forty corpses were discovered in a ditch."
Among them was the young man who had been his
patient.

Haidar came into direct confrontation with the
Israelis when they dismissed the mayor of Gaza, Mu-
nir Rayess, and replaced him with Rushdi A Shawa,
whom they asked to form a municipal council. Haidar
was told he was to be one of the ten members on the
board. The pro-Egyptian doctor was reluctant. "I
thought this out and decided that if I refuse, then they
are going to give this problem to somebody else. Why
should I pass the buck? So I went."

But the two men constantly clashed. "Mr. A

Shawa, the mayor, was rather conciliatory to the Israelis," says Haidar, who refused to give the Israelis
an inch. In an effort to show other countries how they
were allowing self-governance, the Israelis would
bring foreign journalists and diplomats to meet the
council members. While A Shawa would tell them that
life was much better under the Israelis, Haidar would
immediately say it was not. "I would start commend-
ing the Egyptians," he explains. "They called me a
troublemaker." Not long after, Haidar resigned. The
Israelis were furious and responded by cutting off his
electricity and water supply. The Israeli occupation
was short-lived, but the brutality stayed in Haidar's
mind.

With the roads to Egypt now reopened, Haidar
was able to rejoin Hoda Khalidi, and the couple were
wed in the summer of 1957 in a marriage that com-
bined wealth, prestige, and influence. Once again Haidar would work for the Egyptians. Having shown his
loyalty to the new Egyptian leader, Gamal Abdel Nasser, he was appointed director of all the medical services in Gaza, a post he kept until he returned to
private practice in 1960. Haidar admired the Egyptian
president and developed a personal friendship with
him. The two men met several times: "Nasser was
very sincere. By all measures he was a moderate and
reasonable man." Nasser's sense of Arab nationalism
and his work for the Egyptian people were in keeping
with Haidar's own philosophy. But, he says, Nasser
was frustrated in his efforts. "He suffered from a weak
staff and could not cope with all his burdens."

During the 1960s, Haidar watched as Nasser's
ideas of socialism and pan-Arabism flourished: he acquired economic aid from the Soviet Union and built
the Aswan Dam; he supported Arab organizations,
such as the Arab Nationalist Movement; signed pacts
with several Arab nations; and drew Egypt into the
international spotlight. His electrifying personality
put Egypt in the center of the Arab League, and in

1964, under its auspices, the first Palestinian National Congress met in Jerusalem. Haidar Abdul Shafi was sent as a representative to that meeting and helped create the Palestine Liberation Organization. The organization's charter, written at the Jerusalem congress, declared that the aim of the PLO was the elimination of Israel and the creation of a Palestinian state. Haidar was one of only fifteen people appointed to its prestigious Executive Committee.

The man announced as head of the newly formed PLO was Ahmed Shukeiry, the Palestinian guerrilla leader who had represented Syria and Saudi Arabia at the UN. Shukeiry had developed a reputation for spiteful polemics at the World Council, often calling for the physical extermination of all Jews. The embittered Palestinians were only too eager to become Shukeiry's foot soldiers, and the Palestine Liberation Army was formed as the fighting arm of the PLO.

Haidar returned to Gaza and began to balance two priorities—his private practice of routine surgery, and building an infrastructure for the struggle against Israel. Although it may seem that the two areas conflicted, they were actually not incompatible. Through his work as a doctor, Haidar could provide medical care for the poor; in turn, he would receive their loyalty as their debt. He could develop a constituency out of his clinics and establish a political base for himself. When the Executive Committee of the PLO met in Gaza two years later, Haidar had already claimed the leadership of the Strip.

Haidar and his wife had been in Alexandria for several weeks. He had been studying ambulance care; she had been visiting her family. On June 4, 1967, Haidar took a train back to Gaza; it would be the last train to leave from Egypt.

Gaza had an eerie feeling to it when he returned. The crowded streets were deserted, the noisy hordes had been silenced, the cars had come to a stop. "It was a hollow city with all the signs of an emergency," he recalls. At work in his office the next morning, he heard the first explosions. The news reports on the radio announced that the Israelis had struck at the airfields in the Sinai, destroying the Soviet-built jets, and had bombarded the Egyptian units in Gaza. By the next day they had taken over the Strip.

The city was still ghostly quiet, under curfew day and night. Haidar was in Shifa Hospital, working as a volunteer. There was little to do; the pipes had burst and there was not even water for the hospital. "Things looked so desperate," he remembers. Sitting around with the others, Haidar had a premonition that the Israelis might strike at the hospital. Quietly, he and another doctor sneaked out of the building and walked quickly toward his home. Minutes after the two men left, the Israelis charged the hospital and took the doctors into detention. Haidar had escaped, but Gaza had not, and once again it was under Israeli rule. This time the Israelis were there for a long stay.

The PLO was illegal under Israeli law; Haidar, like all Palestinians, was forced to renounce his membership and could only offer verbal support. But the ranks of activists were growing as hatred for the Israelis intensified. With the influx of more refugees after the Six-Day War, Gaza had become one of the most densely populated areas of the world. The majority of its people were still living under the wretched conditions of the camps, and their venom was overflowing like the sewage in the cesspools. The appeal of the PLO was irresistible. Thousands of youths joined its militant wings, such as Fatah, and many joined George Habash's extremist Popular Front for the Liberation of Palestine, an outgrowth of the Arab Nationalist Movement. With the help of Syria, the group was able to arm itself with Kalashnikovs and other weapons and engage in an increasing number of terrorist acts. Haidar, witness to the suffering of his people, and victim once again of the Israeli army, encouraged the goals of the group. Though he says he was not a member of the PFLP, he was considered by the Israelis to be one of its local supporters.

Haidar's contempt for the Israelis was enormous; he would approve of nothing that increased Gaza's dependence on the Jewish state. When the Israelis insisted on replacing the old Egyptian electric generators with new ones of their own, Haider was outraged and protested, claiming that it was one more move to control the Arabs and increase their reliance on Israel. The Israeli in charge of the occupation was the defense minister, Moshe Dayan. Several times the former general called Haidar to try to persuade him to change his mind, but the stubborn doctor would not budge. Just to make sure that Haidar would not sabotage his efforts, Dayan expelled him to a military outpost in the Sinai. That same day Haidar heard an Israeli news report announcing his expulsion and accusing him of collaborating with terrorists. Says Haidar, "It was the first time that I knew they were telling lies." Haidar spent his time in the Bedouin village of Nahal, while the Israelis installed new electrical lines. Three months later, Dayan permitted Haidar to return, certain that now he would not sabotage his own people by having his activists cut off their electricity. Dayan had sent Haidar a message making it clear who was in control.

With no hope in sight of a political solution to grant the Palestinians a homeland, acts of violence were taking place all over the world, aimed at the Israelis, but killing and wounding hundreds of American and European civilians. Orchestrated mainly by the PFLP, terrorist groups had hijacked dozens of commercial airplanes in Europe and the Middle East, taking the passengers as hostages. In addition, Yasser Arafat's Fatah group had carried out sixty different acts of sabotage against the Israelis inside their territory, and thousands more that originated inside Jordan. In Gaza itself, PLO activists conducted a reign

of terror, murdering local Arabs whom they considered collaborators. Anarchy prevailed; shoot-outs between Arab youths and Israeli soldiers took place in
the narrow alleys of the refugee camps. To Haidar's
delight, the Israeli military government had become
paralyzed by the Palestinians.

In June 1970, the Israelis deported six Palestinian
leaders in an effort to stop these activities. Among
them was Haidar Abdul Shafi. This time Haidar was
sent across the border to Lebanon. He was allowed
to return to Gaza three months later, after King Hussein's troops had killed thousands of Palestinian fighters in Jordan. The king had become concerned about
the strength of the terrorists operating in his country
and had sent his army out to destroy them. That sad
day in Palestinian lore, known as Black September,
marked the king as an enemy of the Palestinian fighters and reinforced Haidar's loyalty to Egypt.

The defeat of the guerrillas brought with it the
arousal of religious fundamentalist groups. Strongest
among these was the Moslem Brotherhood, which had
been active underground in Egypt for many years. The
fundamentalists were opposed to the PLO, which they
saw as too political and nationalistic. Delighted by
their anti-PLO position, the Israelis supported the fundamentalists, allowing them to receive financing and
support.

It was the last year that Haidar would see his
friend Nasser, now a man humiliated in defeat. The
Egyptian leader died soon after and was succeeded by
his deputy, Anwar Sadat.

October 6, 1973, was a day that Haidar will always remember. At two o'clock in the afternoon, the
Egyptian and Syrian armies launched surprise attacks
on Israeli camps and installations. The Egyptians followed up by sending thousands of soldiers across the
Suez Canal into the Sinai Desert, while in the north
the Syrians advanced on the Golan Heights. The Israelis had been almost completely undefended: their

soldiers, their generals, and their ministers had all been at home or in synagogue praying. The Israelis were observing their most important holiday, Yom Kippur, the Day of Atonement. The Arabs were celebrating their most important day too—almost certain victory over the Jewish state. For three weeks the war raged on while Egypt and Syria consolidated their positions. The surprise attack, and Israel's inability to repulse it easily, brought waves of pride to Egypt and her supporters. In addition, Jordan's refusal to enter the war with Egypt and Syria cost her further loyalty from the Palestinian community. The PLO took over as official representative of the Palestinians. Once again, Haidar could hold his head high.

But Haidar's pride was soon diminished. Anwar Sadat agreed to a plan drawn up by the American secretary of state, Henry Kissinger; Sadat would disengage Egypt's forces from the Israelis in Sinai in exchange for a cease-fire. Syria too would separate its armies from the Israelis on the Golan Heights, and there was talk in the air that Jordan might even withdraw from the West Bank. Haidar was furious. Egypt had bought a temporary peace, and the cost had been a betrayal of the Palestinians.

Although Haidar was enraged by Sadat's activities, his own stature was enhanced by the increasing influence of the PLO. At a 1974 Arab summit conference in Rabat the Arab leaders declared that the Palestinian people had a right to return to their homeland and a right to self-determination, and they agreed that the PLO was the Palestinians' sole legitimate representative. As a member of the Executive Committee, Haidar gained more importance in Gaza, and his newly acquired position as head of the Red Crescent further increased his power.

The public health situation in Gaza was deplorable. According to a report from the West Bank Data Project, the Israelis had done little to improve the conditions of the hospitals, and medical services were minimal. In Shifa Hospital, the central hospital in Gaza, the few X-ray machines and electrocardiograph units that existed were broken or outmoded. Even worse, its sanitary conditions were abominable. The rooms were filthy, the beds were rusty and covered with blood-stained sheets, and the operating rooms were decaying and littered with cigarette butts. Mice and roaches roamed the halls and visited the patients more frequently than the doctors did.

The Red Crescent could help by supplying out-patient care at its six clinics. In addition, its fleet of ambulances could reach the ill and the elderly and convey them to some sort of medical relief. As a welfare society, the Red Crescent received funds from numerous sources and could channel its money to the poor by offering jobs and other services. As chairman of the organization, Haidar was highly important to the community. But his power was tested once again by Moshe Dayan.

In November 1977, Anwar Sadat reached his hand out to the Israelis and made his historic visit to Jerusalem. Less than a year later Sadat saw a chance to regain the Sinai; he could call Israel's bluff by offering it the one thing it had always been denied, peace. Peace would also mean the end of maintaining the largest army in the Arab world. Egypt had lost eighty thousand soldiers in four wars against Israel. The Egyptian economy was in shambles; its people were hungry and its army demoralized.

The following September, Sadat joined Menachem Begin and signed the Camp David Accords, sealing a peace treaty between Egypt and Israel. The treaty offered the promise of autonomy to the Palestinians, but denied them the guarantees of a state. For Haidar, the Camp David Accords were the ultimate sell-out. Egypt, the most populous and heavily armed Arab nation, the country that he and everyone else looked upon as the leader of the Arab world, had done the unthinkable: it had recognized the Zionist entity and conspired to doom the Palestinian people.

The Palestinians in the West Bank and Gaza responded by forming a National Guidance Committee. Haidar joined with other PLO supporters and wrote the committee's manifesto, stating that there could be no peace without the right of the Palestinians to return to their homeland and establish an independent state with Jerusalem as its capital. In Gaza, Haidar used the Red Crescent to carry out the committee's instructions, dispatching his volunteers to pass out leaflets in the refugee camps condemning Camp David and Anwar Sadat.

The Red Crescent also played a role in transporting people, particularly the students who traveled from Gaza to the free universities in Egypt. Until the Camp David Accords, the Red Crescent had brought the students back and forth, acting as an intermediary between Egypt and Israel. After the signing of the accords, the Israelis informed the Egyptians that an intermediary was no longer necessary. But the Egyptians had not yet fully accepted normal relations and refused to go along with the Israelis. They still wanted the Red Crescent to act as a middleman.

In May 1979, hundreds of Gaza students who had been at school in Egypt were ready to come home for summer vacation. In fact, they had no choice but to come home, since their rooms at the universities had been taken over by the next semester's students. In addition, the university entrance examination papers of seven thousand Gaza students had to be sent to professors in Egypt for grading and approval. Haidar recalls, "The Israelis wanted to pick up the students on the border at El Arish. But the Egyptians refused to collect the examination papers themselves; they insisted that they should be handed to them by the Red Crescent." Haidar was caught in the middle; meanwhile, the students were stranded, and he saw no reason for them to suffer because of the stubbornness of two leaders.

The telephone rang in his office, and it was Moshe Dayan. The defense minister sounded weak, and was calling from the hospital where he had undergone surgery for cancer. Dayan, "always a gentleman and diplomatic," began his conversation by congratulating Haidar on his election as head of the Red Crescent. He quickly followed the compliment by explaining that there was no reason for the Egyptians not to deal directly with the Israelis.

"I understand this, General Dayan, but why should the students suffer because of this misunderstanding?"

"It's not our fault. It's the Egyptians," the general replied.

"We cannot argue your case with the Egyptians," Haidar explained.

The case was not settled, and the following day Dayan sent one of his deputies to discuss the matter further. But Dayan was adamantly opposed to using the Red Crescent, and in the end, says Haidar, "he did not move a millimeter on that issue." The Egyptians finally gave in. "I think logically Israel was right," Haidar concedes.

Several more meetings followed between Haidar and Moshe Dayan, and although the Palestinian praises the Israeli for his efforts to understand the Arab side, he has never forgiven him for being the occupier.

Not long after the incident with the students, the Egyptians canceled the free university education they had been providing to Gazans. "That was shameful," Haidar charges. Instead of the students going to Egypt to study, many would now begin to travel to schools in the West Bank, bringing with them their revolutionary and fundamentalist fervor, which had been building up in the camps.

In Gaza itself, thanks to the generosity of the Israelis, fundamentalism was flourishing. Since the beginning of the occupation in 1967, the Israelis had allowed the Moslems to build more than one hundred mosques and to increase the size of the Islamic University. It was hoped that although the frustrations of the refugees remained, they would have a religious outlet. Unfortunately, their passion took a more vindictive turn, and the growth of the Islamic Jihad, the holy war against Israel, was the result. Even the Red Crescent suffered in its wake. In 1980 a group of students marched from the Islamic University to the headquarters of the Red Crescent and set the building on fire. Successful with their first mission, they raced down the street toward the home of the Shafis. Only seconds before they reached the house, they were stopped by Israeli troops.

The ceramic tiles that form an Arabic design on the floor of the veranda are no longer made. The crystal chandeliers that hang from the high ceilings inside are rarely seen anymore. The Shafis' villa marks an earlier era. Haidar himself seems to embody a previous time. Yet he is not so inflexible that he will not change or adapt to the ways of the present. Sitting on the veranda, looking out on a Gaza under curfew, he says that the Islamic Jihad "has distinguished itself in fighting the occupation."

He knows that in the streets of Gaza women now often wear the veil, and husbands go to the beaches without their wives. He knows that at the university, nearly 80 percent of the students have voted for the Moslem Brotherhood. He knows too that at graduation ceremonies, the young men and women no longer sit together but are divided on opposite sides of a plastic fence. In the classrooms, the women are taught by women, and the men by men.

The Jihad prevails in Gaza. It not only threatens the customs of the people; it threatens the existence of their most important representative, the PLO. Once considered radical, the PLO is now looked upon as moderate, especially when compared to the Moslem Brotherhood. Unless there is movement toward a political settlement, Haidar believes that the fundamentalism fueling the *intifada* soon will be irreversible. The Jihad demands an Islamic state to replace the state of Israel. The PLO and its supporters are willing to accept the establishment of a Palestinian state in the West Bank and Gaza.

Haidar says, "There is no problem of coexistence. The Jewish presence is a reality to be acknowledged."

THE PALESTINIAN GUERRILLA

Two Generations of Fighters

Ahmed Abu Tariq Issawi
and Hanni Issawi

No! I swear by this land,
and thou art a lodger in this land;
by the begetter, and that he begot,
indeed, We created man in trouble.
What does he think none has power over him,
saying, 'I have consumed wealth abundant'?
What, does he think none has seen him?

—THE LAND,
THE KORAN

Ask most Israelis who live in Jerusalem how to get to Issawiya and they will look as if they'd been asked directions to the moon. Issawiya, to be sure, is as psychologically removed from Jerusalem as the lunar body is physically distant from the earth. Yet the fate of the people in this old Arab village is inextricably linked with the destiny of the modern Israeli state.

An Arab friend who knows the way drives
through east Jerusalem, then scornfully turns in at
French Hill, the Jewish enclave that dwarfs the Arab
outskirts of the town. The complex of apartment
houses bears some resemblance to New York's Lefrak
City and other middle-class projects built in the
1950s: block after block of cream-colored buildings
tower over the neighborhood. The road that serves it
is as wide and smooth as in any American suburb.
Cars drive along at a hurried pace, part of the urban
life that has spread beyond the old city limits.

Near the top of French Hill another road turns
slightly to the right and leads up to Mount Scopus.
There, high on the hill above the city, Hadassah Hospital and Hebrew University were built before the war
of 1948, carved out of land bought by the Jews from
the British. But straight ahead, at the end of the road
from French Hill, the paved surface ends, the buildings disappear, and the world seems to come to a halt.
The car continues, bouncing along a rocky path
strewn with rubble.

Here at the desert threshold, where the rain stops
and the fertile green fields give way to the beige sandy
hills, lies the small Arab village of Issawiya. No sign
welcomes outsiders, no pavement smooths the way.
Out of the thick dust that rises from the earth, sand-
colored houses appear here and there, but no street
names or numbers accommodate visitors. Groups of
children, dressed in the blue school uniforms of
UNRWA, walk alongside and gawk into the car: they
know every auto that goes by and recognize an odd
one right away; older boys stand menacingly in the
middle of the road as if to block the vehicle.

This village has been one of the leaders of the
uprising. It is here that the Israelis have found printing
presses that print the leaflets of instruction for the
intifada. For several weeks this town of five thousand
people was under military control, and for several
days it had been under curfew. The rocks in the street

have been hurled at soldiers, and tires have been burned to prevent strangers coming through.

"The house of Ahmed Abu Tariq Issawi?" the driver asks in Arabic and the children are eager to help. Ten of them try to climb inside the car, and the driver must move on quickly before they smother him with curiosity. The road to Ahmed's house is around a bend and up a steep hill, and the small car labors as it struggles to grip the pitted ground. Finally the house comes into view, a pale stone dwelling hidden behind overgrown shrubs and an iron gate. At the sound of the doorbell, a white-haired man appears, dressed neatly in light blue pants and a matching shirt that sets off his white mustache and suntanned face. He looks younger than his eighty years, and his body is still that of the rebel who fought in the mountains so long ago. "Welcome, you are welcome," says Ahmed Abu Tariq Mustafa Issawi; welcome to the home of the village chief.

"I, my father, my grandfather, and my grand grandfather were all born here," the old man says with aristocratic pride. "They owned most of the lands of the village." He leads you to the veranda of his spacious house and points to the dry brown hills that stretch for miles around, from the edges of Jerusalem to the road to Jericho. Above the house stands Mount Scopus; behind it French Hill, once part of the two thousand acres farmed by his people. Way beyond lie fields and caves that served as hiding places for his children and burial grounds for the Jewish people two thousand years ago. Generation after generation of Ahmed's family have handed down this land from father to son and from father to son.

Since the days of the Ottoman Empire, the Issawi clan has ruled the village, employing its people to cultivate the fields with lentils, corn, barley, and other crops; advising its men in their daily squabbles and struggles to survive; leading its youth in fiery battles against the endless stream of foreign rulers. From this two-story house flew the neutral flag of the United Nations from 1948 to 1967, protecting the village from the Jordanians and the Israelis. In this home was Issawiya's only telephone, for nineteen years the area's sole connection to the outside world.

Ahmed moves inside to the tile-floored living room and relaxes in an overstuffed brown chair. Around the room are pictures of some of his ten children: Osama, killed in a battle in the Baka'a Valley in southern Lebanon; Razi, who lives in the U.S. and is not allowed back home; daughter Rihab, a teacher who has been imprisoned for helping the *intifada*; and his son Hanni, a guerrilla who was imprisoned for ten years by the Israelis. He is proud of his son who was martyred for the Palestinian cause and boasts of the others who have gone to prison; like him, they are fighters for their people.

Ahmed traces his own heroics back to 1936, when he led a revolutionary group against the British rulers. His handful of guerrilla fighters were easy targets for the aircraft that swept the hills in search of the Arab enemy. But Ahmed would outsmart the English. Under cover of dusk, he would lead his men from their hidden caves to attack, then make a hasty retreat to the mountains, disappearing in the shadows of the sunset. Skirmish after skirmish was fought in the hills from Hebron to Nablus, and for three years he helped to keep the battles going. Three times he was condemned to death by hanging, and twenty-three times he served time in prison, shuffled between the British in Egypt and Iraq, and the French in Syria and Lebanon. Always he was able to return home, and always he was a hero to the people of Issawiya.

After the British left the area, and the war was fought between Israel and the Arabs in 1948, Issawiya became a convoluted neutral ground: physically part of the Israelis' enclave of Mount Scopus, which had been turned into a military base; technically under the

Jordanians' control of east Jerusalem and the West Bank; and in actuality maintained as a no-man's-land by the United Nations. From 1948 to 1967 the white-and-blue UN flag flew from the rooftop of the most important house in the village, the home of Ahmed Abu Tariq. Under its neutral watch he raised his ten children, seven sons and three daughters, passing on to them the rich heritage of his family's command in the belief that he would pass on the land as his father, Ali, passed it on to him, and his father, Mohammed, before him, and his father before him.

But the Israelis interrupted his plans. After their victory over Jordan in 1967, when they annexed east Jerusalem and reunited the city, Issawiya became a part of the Israeli capital. In the process, the Israelis confiscated Arab property all around—the first time that an outside ruler had actually taken land from the people. The fields of Issawiya began to shrink, two hundred acres taken at one time, another two hundred acres taken at a later date. After a few years, only five hundred of the original twenty-five hundred acres were left.

In return for the land, the Israelis offered money, lots of money. "They told me, 'If you work with us, instead of staying in Jerusalem during the summers, you can be in the south of France or Paris or London,' " recalls Ahmed, who says a quarter of an acre is now worth eighty thousand dollars.

"But I replied, 'Why didn't you tell me that before, when I was younger? Now I am too old to go.' And the Israelis said, 'Take the money, any amount of money you want.'

"I told them, 'If I took the money in place of the land, then I could not raise my head. What could I do if I stood before anyone, even after death? When we are standing before God, and God asks my grandfather, 'Where is the land, Mohammed?' My grandfather will say, 'I gave it to my son Ali.'

"And when God asks Ali, 'Where is the land that your father gave you?' He will say, 'I gave it to Ahmed.'

"And when He asks me, 'Where is the land that your father gave you?' I will not be crestfallen. I will say, 'I gave it to my son, but the government took it.' And my head will still be raised."

The former Israeli official who offered the money to Ahmed and to other Arabs in east Jerusalem still recalls the incident. Says Meron Benvenisti, "I was ready to negotiate any way he wanted. When the land was confiscated, I tried to offer them money so at least they didn't lose." If the Arabs did not want to recognize the confiscation, then they didn't have to. "But at least they were not losing anything," says Benvenisti. "If things changed, and they got back the land, then they would have the land and the money. But for them, it is a matter of principle."

The Israeli acknowledges that Ahmed was not alone: although a few Arabs sold their land privately to settlers, not a single Arab whose land was confiscated accepted payment in return. "They could all have been wealthy," says Benvenisti, "but they think that the owner is not for sale. And I accept that."

Ahmed's son Hanni, born in 1952, reflects the valiant image of his father. With thick black hair and mischievous dark eyes, slight build and lightning-quick legs, he is the modern counterpart of the elder Issawi, a man who maneuvers around the enemy and prides himself on the battles he has fought. A child raised on stories of bloody struggles and the righteousness of war, Hanni loved to hear his father's tales of conflict with the British. As an adolescent he was roused by his brothers' reports of Palestinian fighters and their courageous clashes with the Jews. His own first encounter with a foreign army came at the age of fourteen: the daring schoolboy and his friends tried to demonstrate against their ruler, Jordan, for not protecting the Palestinians from the Jews. But the struggle didn't last long when the soldiers surrounded the students and quickly shut their school.

A year later, in the spring of 1967, the talk of Arab-Israeli war filled the air. By late May the stage was set: Egyptian forces had crossed the Suez Canal into the Sinai Desert, joined a few days later by Algerian and Kuwaiti troops; the armies of Jordan and Iraq were put under Egyptian command; and President Nasser announced he was going to destroy the Jewish state. Like everyone else he knew, fifteen-year-old Hanni hoped that the Jordanians would win. After all, they were Arabs also, and perhaps they would help his people regain their land.

As Hanni and his family sat on the veranda of their house on the morning of June 5, they heard the first explosions of the war. With their unobstructed view of Mount Scopus they could see the Jordanian bombs falling on Hadassah. Excited and buoyed with hope, they cheered the Jordanians on. "It was a direct attack," says Hanni. But disappointment followed fast. "We noticed that when they hit Hadassah, all we could see was a lot of smoke and no destruction." Soon after, Israeli bombs were flaring from Hadassah back toward Jordan. With their ears glued to the radio, the family listened in amazement as the Jordanians announced they had destroyed the Jewish military outpost. "We were sitting there, and we saw that Hadassah was shooting at the villages," says Hanni. "Yet on the radio, we heard that Hadassah was finished."

For four days, from Monday till Thursday, the family watched as the war continued, bombs bursting above them and around them; but save for a few bullets that hit the wall of their house, the village was hardly touched.

On Thursday morning the family awakened to the harsh sound of shouting through loudspeakers. Leave your houses or be vulnerable to attack, the Israelis called in Arabic to the people of Issawiya. With no air-raid shelters to protect them, and nowhere else to hide, the Issawiyans gathered some belongings and set off. Only those too old or too ill to leave stayed behind. Led by Ahmed, who was head of the village council, Hanni, eight of his brothers and sisters, their mother, and the others trekked off on the road to Jericho, where they knew they could hide in the ancient caves. The family shared a putrid cavern with cows and goats and stayed up half the night in fear of snakes.

In the morning light the villagers convened and, with Ahmed as their council chief, decided to return to Issawiya. They would not repeat the Arab flights of 1948. Better to die in their homes, they agreed, than to die as refugees outside. With his expertise as a guerrilla fighter, Ahmed sneaked back alone to Issawiya to make sure that it was safe. Hours later, when he returned to the caves, he laid out a careful plan: each family would make its way back alone by a separate route; some might be attacked along the way, but at least not all of the villagers would be doomed.

Slowly the families made their way home and found the village had been searched, house by house, room by room. They were ordered under curfew; for several days they were allowed out for only a few hours to harvest the fields. Not long after, the sound of loudspeakers pierced the village once again as the Israelis called for a gathering of all the men. Every male over the age of eighteen was ordered to the center of town; the soldiers demanded the weapons that the villagers had kept hidden from the Jordanians. Screams of pain echoed through the town; those who did not obey were badly beaten. Many, like Tariq Issawi, Hanni's older brother, withstood interrogation and refused to give in.

Despite the occupation, after a while life went along as it had before; Hanni went to Rashidiya High

School in Jerusalem, helped with the planting of the crops at home, and once in a while, rode through the fields of Issawiya on his Arabian horse. But Hanni and the others had come face to face with the new enemy, and it forced a change in their thinking: no longer were they only Arabs; now they were aware of being Palestinians.

From time to time the students in Hanni's school would demonstrate, shouting at the Israelis for taking some of their West Bank land. The soldiers would answer, hurling tear gas at the crowds of boys and squirting them with red dye to mark the guilty ones. Later they would search the streets and find the instigators; but Hanni was fast and always able to run away.

On one carefree afternoon Hanni was riding on horseback through the fields, when in the distance he saw an Israeli bulldozer clearing his family's crops, preparing the soil for concrete. "They had started working on French Hill," he recalls. "And I understood from that time, this is not just occupation. It's to be or not to be, to exist or not; because for us, as villagers, we exist to take care of the land."

The Israelis were doing what no previous invader had dared to do; neither the Jordanians, nor the British, nor the Turks had taken away their land. Although the occupiers had levied heavy taxes and demanded loyalty, they had always allowed the people to keep their farms. But now the Palestinians of Issawiya, like those all along the West Bank, were losing their most vital possession: the very earth that gave them their food and their pride and made them who they were.

Hanni Issawi rose quietly from his bed and quickly put on the clothes he had set aside earlier. Under the cover of darkness, he slipped out of the house, praying that no one in the family would see him or hear him. His heart beat fast as he hurried along the dirt path, following the way he knew well to the caves outside the village. For six months now he had been stealing out of the house late at night, well after his parents and his brothers were asleep, joining the others in the group. Of course, his father would never be angry with him; he'd be proud of his eighteen-year-old son for being the youngest of the ten men in the cell. Still, he had taken an oath and he had to keep the group a secret from everyone. He knew that they had watched him for a long time before they invited him to join, first making sure that he was brave enough and truly devoted to the Palestinian cause. Hanni had come to a conclusion in his last year in school that the only way to stop the Israeli aggression was by fighting; he had decided to join the revolution. He was thrilled when they had asked him to be part of the *fedayeen*, the Fatah guerrillas who vowed to fight by any means. His code name was Abu Haithen.

Almost every night they would practice hiding in the mountains and the caves. He never felt afraid; he was too thrilled to care. He knew that the Israelis were too frightened to venture near the caves, and he felt strong having weapons in his hands. Each time he went, he learned a little more: how to use a sub-machine gun, how to carry it, how to throw a hand grenade. Hanni had seen a pistol before, of course, but never anything like these Czechoslovakian Samosars that had been found in the caves. Wasn't it like the Jordanians to run in fear from the Israelis in '67 and leave their weapons behind!

Twice now the group had made successful attacks with the weapons, and the news had made the front pages of the papers: in May 1970 they had thrown two hand grenades inside the Hazvi restaurant in Jerusalem and wounded nine civilians; four months later, in September, they had tossed two more grenades at the famous Dolphin restaurant, killing one person and injuring fifteen others. Only two or three group members went together to make an assault, and Hanni had not been asked to go. Besides, he had said he was against attacking civilians. But there would be other times, other chances.

The group was upset when they lost their supply connection in Jordan. Such great plans they had had for sneaking weapons across the border! Then came that day called Black September, when King Hussein's troops massacred some twenty thousand Palestinians fighting for their nationalist cause. Now they could not bring in the weapons as they had hoped to do; nevertheless, they still had ammunition for more attacks. At least they still had enough for their plan to blow up an Israeli Egged bus.

Tonight they talked about their scheme to strike at the border guards in Ramallah, and Hanni was eager to go. Soon, they told him, soon.

On November 19, 1970, Hanni lay in his bed listening to the heavy whirring sound outside. He knew what was happening, but there was nowhere he could hide, no one who could help him. He crept out to the veranda and looked up; it was two A.M. and the sky was filled with helicopters, the mountains crawling with soldiers. The Israelis had found out about the weapons from a collaborator in the group and had surrounded the village. Hanni went back inside the house and slipped into his bed. He would wait. What else could he do?

The knock was loud and he went and opened the door himself. The border guards were standing outside; the Shin Bet was at the door.

Hanni Issawi, they asked for. We have come to arrest him.

I am Hanni, he told them, but they didn't believe him. You are too small and too young, they said.

His older brother came, and they asked him for his ID card. Then they asked the little one for his card, too. When they saw that it really was Hanni, they took him away and brought him to Moscobiya, the central police station, for interrogation. One month later he and the others were put on trial, and three judges heard the case: Ammon Allon, Aram Alparon, and Yoshua Ben Zion, a supporter of the settlement movement.

They called him a terrorist.

"I am not a terrorist, I am a guerrilla fighting for a cause."

They charged him on ten counts, the most serious ones for hiding weapons and for carrying ammunition: a pistol, thirteen bullets, and a hand grenade. Only he and one of the others knew where the rest of the weapons were hidden.

"I didn't kill anyone," he told them.

It didn't matter, they said. He was a member of the group, knew about their actions, and didn't try to stop them: twenty-four innocent people were injured and one innocent person was dead.

The Israelis forced this on us, he thought. They used violence and terrorism to deny us our rights as Palestinians. What we are doing is just answering their way.

Twelve years in prison, they said.

But even now, to Hanni and his father, Ahmed, there was no other way. "For people who want their rights back, any means of resistance is justified," says the son, "especially with an enemy who uses violence as a means to control people."

The Israelis are terrorists too, he says, throwing tear gas, beating youths, and shooting rubber bullets at demonstrators whose only weapons are rocks and gasoline bombs. And when the Israelis raze the homes of Arab villagers, even of those who are directly involved in violence, this is terrorism, too.

"The best way is by negotiation," he acknowledges. "We know that using violence and using weapons is going to deepen the struggle between the two nationalities, the Israelis and the Palestinians, but the violence was forced on me."

For the first four years in the Ramle prison, Hanni was permitted to leave his cell for just one hour every day. His only activity was reading, and his only reading matter was the books and newspapers provided by the Israelis. The best way to use his time, he decided, was to learn Hebrew; and with a dictionary by his side, Hanni taught himself the language. Before long he was translating books about the Arabs from Hebrew into Arabic and giving them to the other prisoners. "In jail, life was to cooperate," he says. "Whatever you have, you give to the others."

In 1974, to the surprise of Hanni and his friends, a new prisoner arrived in the wards. Yoshua Ben Zion, the judge who had sentenced him, was convicted of embezzling $47 million from the British-Israeli Bank. When Hanni saw the Gush Emunim judge, he asked for his help in reducing his term in jail. "If there was justice," he explains, "all the cases which he ruled would have been tried again." But Ben Zion could hardly help. "I am in a position where I can only hope for you to have a good life," said the former judge. "I can't do anything else right now." Nevertheless, Hanni's sentence was reduced by two years after a court decided that he had not owned the weapons he was charged with hiding.

His ten-year stay in prison served as a training ground for his future life. He strengthened his ties with pro-PLO and other more radical agitators, deepened his commitment to the Palestinian cause, educated himself, and even laid the groundwork for jobs when he was released from jail. He became a leader, joined a committee to negotiate between the prisoners and the authorities, and gained influence with his fellow Palestinians. In response, the Israelis moved him around to several different prisons, a hopeless attempt to break up the closely knit networks formed inside the jails.

In a final endeavor to suppress him and other leaders, the Israelis sent Hanni to Nafha, a prison in the distant Negev, where conditions were harsher than before: the scalding heat of the desert sun, the confiscation of his books, the tiny prison yard, and the lack of visitors made life nearly intolerable. Once again, Hanni became part of a committee to negotiate with the Israeli authorities, but this time his efforts failed.

As a back-up move, he helped organize another type of protest. On July 14, Bastille Day, in honor of the French revolutionaries, Hanni and the others began a hunger strike. For thirty-three days the prisoners refused to eat; the Israelis refused to negotiate. Desperate to keep the prisoners alive, the Israelis transferred them back to the hospital at Ramle, where they fed them by force. But rather than feeding them the required glass of milk and an egg, the doctors experimented, inserting tubes of salt water into their lungs. As Hanni lay in bed, weak and dehydrated, two of his fellow prisoners died from suffocation. Hanni's older sister, Ribah, director of a Quaker school, was called back from a conference in Greece; Hanni was hours away from death.

The prisoners' deaths caused a scandal in Israel, and on August 16 the Israeli interior minister announced on the radio that the authorities had agreed to give in to the prisoners' demands. Hanni and the others in the hospital had not heard the news; even when the doctors told them, they still refused to eat. Only the appearance of one of his comrades, sent from Nafha to assure him, convinced Hanni that the strike was over.

Four months later Hanni was released and brought to his home in Issawiya. The house was filled with flowers, and his relatives greeted him with songs and dancing. But no, he said, and quickly stopped the celebration. He could not forget his comrades who were still suffering in jail. That night he slept in his sister Ribah's bedroom; when he awoke early the next morning, Ribah watched in silent disbelief as Hanni checked the window of the bedroom door to see if there were prison guards outside. Slowly and cautiously, he opened the door and looked in the hallway, making sure that it was safe to leave the room. Says Ribah, "I felt so sad when I saw that. I will never forget that scene."

In the tradition of Palestinian prisoners, Hanni was treated as a hero and taken care of by his fellow activists, who arranged for him to have a job. In 1982 he opened his own office as a translator, earning a bit of money translating birth certificates and other official documents. But his main work was to translate Hebrew newspapers into Arabic and sell the information to the Arab press. Within three months the Israelis shut his office. Three years later he tried once more, this time working as a translator for a friend: four months went by and the Israelis shut the office again.

In 1987 he opened a business for journalists, translating Hebrew articles into Arabic for the pro-PLO news magazine *Al-Awdah*, and for the Israeli Marxist newspaper *Al-Sharara*, "The Way of the Spark." In December of that year, with the start of the *intifada*, he began acting as a link between the Palestinians and the foreign press. His role became more important: he received information from the uprising's network and provided it to reporters covering the story. For the first heated month he served as a useful liaison, taking tips from his well-informed sources on where and when the *intifada* action would occur and feeding the information to the eager reporters from the United States and Europe. But the

Israeli government soon stepped in. In January 1988
he was put under six months' administrative detention
and returned to the Ramle jail.

To the Israelis, even this was hardly punishment.
With its TV lounge, radios in every cell, and plethora
of books, Ramle, they told him, was little more than
a change of address. When they discovered his connection to the Israeli communists, they transferred
him to a harsher prison, Petah Tikvah, and interrogated him for almost a month. But at the trial Hanni
charmed the judge, who said she could not believe he
was as dangerous as he was made out to be.

Now, four days after he has been released, he is
bathing in the glory of his heroism. Friends come to
the house to congratulate him, and his mother plies
him with sweets and cakes. As for his political beliefs,
Hanni says, "The best way is to live with the Jews in
one democratic state." For the moment, he acknowledges, his goal is difficult to achieve. "So the solution
would be having two separate states now, and maybe
we will reach one state in the end."

In the meantime he and his family in Issawiya will
support the *intifada* with any means at hand. His sister
Ribah, who has been jailed for carrying leaflets, de-
fends the uprising despite her Quaker training.
"Stones are not violent," she states. Hanni talks about
the Palestinians accused of violence against the settlers
and says it is the Israelis who are the provocateurs.
"The Palestinians use stones or knives," he says. "The
settlers use machine guns." Their father, Ahmed, de-
fends their struggle at all cost. "Life is a battle," he
says. "Don't try to leave the battle. It is better to die
standing than to die kneeling and better to die kneeling than to die crawling."

THE PALESTINIAN ELITE

The Legacy of Leadership

Faisal Husseini

Surely upon Us rests the guidance,
and to Us belong the Last and the First.
—THE NIGHT,
THE KORAN

The phone call from his close friend came only a day after Faisal Husseini was released from jail. In his quiet voice Faisal answered the phone and listened with surprise to Sari Nusseibeh's suggestion that he meet with a member of the Likud party. Is he serious? Faisal wanted to know. Does he speak for the government? His friend answered in the affirmative. Good, then let's get together, said the prominent Palestinian, and the rendezvous was arranged.

The secret meeting took place in August 1987 at the east Jerusalem home of Sari Nusseibeh, professor at Bir Zeit University and son of the former defense minister of Jordan. The cast of characters was implausible: Palestinians and Israelis representing the extreme from each point of view, the leading roles assigned to Moshe Amirav, a member of the Central Committee of the right-wing Herut party and a close friend of Herut leaders in Yitzhak Shamir's conservative Likud government; and Faisal Husseini, a childhood protégé of Yasser Arafat's and a leading supporter of the PLO in the occupied territories. No one was to know: the very idea of the rendezvous was heretical—that it was actually taking place could destroy them all.

The distinguished-looking Faisal, with his pale skin, dark eyes, and salt-and-pepper hair, chatted amiably with the Israeli-born Amirav. The low-keyed Palestinian could speak Hebrew, learned years past in prison, but the language of choice on this occasion was English; after some pleasantries, the conversation turned to the subject at hand. Faisal, scion of one of the most elite Palestinian families, head of the Arab Studies Society, member of the Waqf, the Moslem religious endowment, son of the leading Arab commander against the Israelis in the war of 1948, grandson and great grandson of mayors of Jerusalem, grandnephew of the grand mufti of Jerusalem, and distant cousin of Yasser Arafat, sat back in his chair and listened as Amirav spoke. The Israeli had written a list of points, the kind of points that the Palestinian had been making for years, the kind of points that had put him in jail three times and kept him under town arrest for seven years. Never a man to reveal all his thoughts, Faisal showed no expression as he heard the words, but inside he was hardly calm: he had worked all his life for a breakthrough like this; maybe now it would all pay off.

Faisal Husseini was born with the consciousness of Palestine and the commitment to bring his country into being. Soft-spoken but staunch in his beliefs, he carries the blood of generations who claim direct descendance from the prophet Mohammed, who have led the Moslem people in Jerusalem and ruled them in the city's affairs. Rich, powerful, and influential, the Husseinis were granted the role of leading family from the days of the Ottoman Empire to the end of the British mandate. Since the seventeenth century, when one of their clan was appointed the mufti of Jerusalem, the highest authority on Moslem law, the Husseinis have been an important family in the city. Since the nineteenth century they have been predominant: they have controlled the Waqf; they have controlled the Arab High Committee; they have controlled the mayoralty; and they have controlled the land, accumulating large parcels of property from the outskirts of Ramallah to the center of the holy city.

To both the Palestinians in the occupied territories and to many Israeli leaders, Faisal is the legitimate indigenous leader, the man who has inherited the legacy of command. But the tall, stoop-shouldered Faisal also bears the weight of fallen aristocracy: to his family goes the blame of a Palestine lost; to his name goes the burden of defeat.

At the end of the nineteenth century the Husseini family moved from the overcrowded Old City to the east Jerusalem neighborhood of Wadi-Joz. There, graceful buildings reflected the colonial style, and land was available to buy and build on. The American Colony Hotel, once the fabulous home of a Turkish pasha and his three wives, sits on property owned by Faisal's grandfather. Next door, a small cemetery protects the graves of Husseini family members. Close by, the New Orient House, built by the Husseini family a few decades ago, is home to the Arab Studies Society. From his offices at the society, its chairman and founder, Faisal Husseini, directs the affairs of state.

The society itself, funded by worldwide sources that range from rich Palestinian refugees, to Arab gov-

ernments, to gifts from the Ford Foundation, acts as
an umbrella organization for Palestinian issues: its
specialized library has books and documents on the
Arab-Israeli conflict and collects magazines and newspapers pertaining to Palestinian and Israeli current
events; its statistical department collects data on different aspects of life under Israeli occupation; its research center conducts research and holds lectures on
Israeli and Palestinian society; its publishing arm
prints books that champion Palestinian martyrs; its
map division prints charts of the settlements in the
West Bank and Gaza and produces maps of Palestine
in its pre-Israeli days; its childhood research center
introduces to preschool teachers new techniques for
conveying the Palestinian identity; its human-rights
center reports Israeli violations to Amnesty International and supports the activities of the *intifada*; its
payroll provides jobs for guerrilla fighters who are
former prisoners.

Less than a year after Faisal established the society, the Israelis tried to put a clamp on his activities,
first refusing him permission to leave the country, then
putting him under a seven-year order of town arrest.
In 1987, at the end of the town arrest, they put him
in prison for three months, then released him and
imprisoned him again for six months more.

The Israelis accuse the society of being a front for
the PLO. They accuse Husseini of opening the institute "for the glorifying and legitimizing of terrorism."
One official says his books turn terrorists who have
killed innocent Israeli children into "glorious martyrs," and adds, "He employs many ex-terrorists and
uses them to intimidate Palestinians." The Israeli mentions Elias Freij, the mayor of Bethlehem, and others
who are willing to act independently of the PLO. "All
one of Husseini's employees has to do is ring Freij's
doorbell and say, 'Good morning.' The rest goes without saying," explains the Israeli, who says Husseini's
people will burn a car or bomb a shop to get their

point across. Says another official about Husseini's role in the territories, "Faisal is the executive producer of the PLO."

Seven-year-old Faisal Husseini sat with his two brothers in their house in Cairo cleaning their new toys. Carefully, Faisal took apart the old weapons, then brushed away the grime built up since World War II. He lovingly applied a slick of oil, then put the parts together, making sure the barrel was spotless. Just like their father and his friends, the boys rubbed and rubbed the tommy gun and the Sten gun and the British Bren until the machine guns were as shiny as their father's glossy boots. How proud young Faisal felt helping his father! How happy he was to have his father home again! Abdul Kader al-Husseini had been away for several months, off again in another country, fighting the war. All his young life Faisal had heard of his father's bravery, leading the commandos against the British in Palestine, struggling in the revolution in Iraq, and now again in Jerusalem, fighting the Jews. Abdul Kader al-Husseini was a true hero—the only member of the Husseini family and the only member of the Arab elite who chose to fight with weapons rather than with words.

From 1936 to 1939, Abdul Kader had commanded guerrilla gangs against the British, fighting desperately for an independent Arab Palestine. The revolt, organized by his uncle Haj Amin, the grand mufti of Jerusalem, had begun with a general strike, had grown to violent riots, and had nearly turned into a revolution. After three years of bloody struggle, Abdul Kader was wanted by the British and had slipped out of the country. His family had been forced to flee to Iraq, leaving their large homes and vast properties under the watchful eye of other relatives, but taking with them the status of leadership. They set up home in Baghdad, where Faisal was born less than a year later. But the elder Husseinis were soon in trouble there too, this time fighting on the side of the Nazis against the British army.

Young Faisal knew well the stories of his father trying to sneak across the border from Iraq to Iran, and how his father had been caught and arrested, and then how he took the family to live in Saudi Arabia. For the little boy those were wonderful days in Arabia—the only times he could remember when his father was at home, spending long hours with the children, even teaching them to read and write because there were no appropriate schools for them in Saudi Arabia.

On January 1, 1946, the family set off once again, this time to Egypt, to be welcomed by King Farouk. In Cairo they would meet up with their uncle, the grand mufti, who had traveled to Syria and to Germany, where he had aligned himself with the fascists and signed an agreement with Adolf Hitler to provide Arab soldiers to fight for the Nazi cause. Haj Amin was highly respected by the Arabs for his leadership in Moslem affairs, and even more so for his avowal to destroy any Zionist state. Together with Hitler and Mussolini, he was certain he could carry out his plans and eliminate the Jews living in Palestine. Even in exile, Haj Amin was the most important leader of Palestinian nationalism; and in Cairo, many prominent Arabs would come to see him and to visit Abdul Kader too. Every day there were friends and relatives being welcomed in Faisal's house.

Almost from the time they arrived in Egypt, Faisal and his brothers saw little of their father. Abdul Kader was always coming and going, traveling to far-away places, recruiting young men as guerrilla fighters, acquiring weapons for their struggle against the partition of Palestine. Faisal knew that the machine guns he was cleaning were precious to his father, that his father needed them badly if he and his men were to win the war against the Jews.

To Faisal the word "war" seemed exciting and rather vague, something like playing with the weapons he and his brothers had cleaned. But when one day the family learned that a cousin they all knew well had been killed, he noticed how his mother became sad. "We started to understand what is war, what is the price of war," he recalls. Still, life went on in their big house in Cairo, and the war in Palestine was very far away. In early April 1948, things changed.

The battle in Palestine was heating up, but so far the Arabs were still winning; they controlled most of Palestine, while the Jewish enclaves were under siege. Especially vulnerable was Jerusalem, and there the Jews were fighting desperately. The Arabs had many more arms and supplies; they had plenty of water, control of the electricity, and in effect, they controlled the city.

Yet the Jews were going on the offensive; rumors were flying that at the very beginning of April they had received two large shipments of arms, several hundred light machine guns and thousands of rifles, sent secretly from Czechoslovakia. Now the Jews were attempting to take over the corridor from Tel Aviv to Jerusalem. On the eastern side, their Haganah fighters had blown up the Ramle headquarters of Hassan Salameh, the mufti's commander in the area, killing some of his most important men. Next, on the western side of the corridor, the Jews had captured the Arab village of Kastel, an old Roman fortress high up in the hills five miles west of Jerusalem, vital because it controlled the approach to the city.

Abdul Kader was in Damascus when he received an urgent call to return to Jerusalem: he was badly needed to command the operations around Kastel. Rushing back to the city, he immediately took control, leading his men in six days and nights of nonstop combat, winning ground around the corridor until the battle was confined to the tiny village. After several more hours of fighting, the Arabs were sure of victory and watched with joy as the Jews retreated from Kastel, ducking the bullets as they fled. In the dim light of early dawn, three Arab fighters walked confidently toward the command post in the center of the enclave. Above them they heard a voice call out, half in English, half in Arabic, "Come on, *yah gamaa*."

"Hello, boys," the Arabs called back in English.

But unbeknownst to them, the Jews were still in control of the command post: the sentry had thought they were Israeli reinforcements. Realizing his mistake, he began to fire; the sputter of machine guns blasted from the post, killing the three men. For days the Israelis were unaware of whom they had killed. But the Arabs knew they had lost their hero: one of the three men was their commander, Abdul Kader.

The solemn funeral of the Palestinian hero was the largest in the history of Jerusalem. Thousands of Arabs, including the troops who had fought so hard for him at Kastel, came to pay their respects to Abdul Kader al-Husseini. But in a terrible turn of events, the Jews recaptured the village in their absence, and the battle for Jerusalem was lost.

"I was at home and my elder brother, Moussa, came to me with the Egyptian newspaper," recalls Faisal Husseini. "Read the headline," the ten-year-old Moussa told him.

When he did, his brother asked, "Do you understand what it says?"

Faisal nodded and answered yes.

"Then go tell your younger brother," Moussa said, and the eight-year-old Faisal went off to tell his little brother, Raisa, that their father was dead.

For three days Faisal felt nothing about his father's death, but when he was shown a newspaper story that the Egyptian government would take care of his family and provide them with free schooling, the little boy started to cry. "In that very moment, I felt the first real thing—not that my father was killed in the war, that it was a national thing and he is a hero, but that I lost my father."

The tradition of leadership was inbred. Moussa immediately moved to his father's place at the table and took over the family responsibilities, even making the arrangements to pay the rent. Faisal was given the role of family spokesman, and on the occasions of memorials for his father, held in various places around Egypt, the young boy was asked to lead the singing of a well-known song written by his father. Composed as a conversation between a child and his mother, the lyrics said, "Talk to me about the land; is it right that the Zionists got our land? Give me my sword, Mother, and I will go and fight for our land."

"When I was reading this, the people would feel as if Abdul Kader Husseini is seeing the future," says Faisal.

The young boy would stand before the gatherings of Egyptian notables and hundreds of Palestinian refugees, leading them in his father's words. "When I was nine years old I was more courageous than when I was thirty or forty years old," Faisal says with a laugh. For six years he would sing the song of his father, but at the age of fifteen he showed the makings of a leader, writing his own poem and delivering it to important Egyptian officials, like Mohammed Nagib, and to the Palestinians.

A day or two before these ceremonial events, a distant cousin and close friend of the family would come to coach him. His name was Abdul Rahman al-Husseini, or as he was known by his friends, Yasser Arafat. The teenaged Arafat had worked diligently for Faisal's father, organizing students at Cairo University and, after he left the school, fighting under his command in Jerusalem. After the war against Israel, Arafat returned to Cairo and became head of the Palestinian Student League. The young Palestinian revolutionary maintained close ties to the Husseini family. "In those days he would visit us at home from time to time, and I started to know him more and more," says Faisal, acknowledging that Arafat had a special fondness for him.

Despite Faisal's father's death, the Husseinis still lived a privileged life in Egypt, spending the school years in Cairo and the summers in their real home, Jerusalem. Faisal finished high school in 1958, the same year that President Nasser announced the United Arab Republic, linking Egypt and Syria in a pan-Arab movement; it was an idea that brought enthusiastic cheers and hearty applause from Faisal, his grand-uncle Haj Amin, and millions of others in the Arab world. It was the same year that a new underground guerrilla organization came into being. Called Fatah, an acronym for the *Palestine Liberation Movement* in reverse, the organization coined the term "Palestinian revolution," reinforcing the concept of a Palestinian identity. Spurred on by the pan-Arab crusade that, it was hoped, would lead to a united Palestine, and by Fatah's slogan of Palestinian nationalism, Faisal felt the spirit of his father's soldierly legend and went off to study in Baghdad at his father's alma mater, the military school. But in Iraq he encountered a revolution to overthrow the monarchy, which prevented his stay in that country. Nine months later he returned to Egypt and took up the fight for Palestine in another way, this time as an activist in the Palestinian Student League.

Although Arafat had since moved on to become a leader in Fatah's new secret fighting cells, Husseini continued his work with the youth group. He organized university students who arrived from the Arab world, Palestinians carrying passports from Jordan, Syria, and Iraq, and refugees from Gaza. Husseini reinforced their consciousness of their Palestinian heritage, holding lectures "about our homeland, our hopes, and our history," he recalls, "trying to make them feel that we are one people." Under the umbrella of Nasser's pan-Arabism, the organization grew broader and more influential. Soon the league was holding conferences with Palestinian students in other Arab countries and as far away as Europe. In 1960 they announced the General United Palestinian Students, an organization of youths from all over the world that would feed the ranks of Fatah.

After three years of a tenuous relationship, the feelings between Egypt and Syria had soured, and in 1961 the United Arab Republic fell apart. The split between the countries came as a blow to Faisal: "All of a sudden I discovered that all our work toward Arab unity, which would lead us toward Palestine, just collapsed. I was working for the Egyptians within an Egyptian structure, and for the Syrians within a Syrian structure; but we, the Palestinians, where were we?" Faisal, like many other young Palestinians, began to ally himself with the ideas of Arafat and Fatah.

As the Palestinian spirit of nationalism grew in strength, and as Fatah and other combat groups began their violent activities against the Israelis, the Arab countries were forced to take notice of the Palestinian cause. In 1964 the Arab League, a loose confederation of fourteen Arab countries including Egypt, Jordan, Syria, Iraq, and Lebanon, established a political body to deal directly with the problem and called it the Palestine Liberation Organization. The PLO's founding congress took place in May 1964 in Jordanian-annexed east Jerusalem; the organization's charter called for the destruction of the Zionist state and for the establishment of a Palestinian entity. The Arab League chose the word *entity* as a concession to the Egyptians and the Jordanians, who felt that a sovereign Palestinian state would threaten their own existence. Faisal Husseini immediately went to work for the PLO in its east Jerusalem headquarters, first at the Ambassador Hotel and then at the UNRWA building nearby.

The bugle call of the Palestine Liberation Army, formed as the fighting arm of the PLO but kept under each member nation's army, was too strong for Faisal to resist. Once again he followed his father's legend, putting aside the world of words for the more potent world of weapons. In 1966 he left for Syria, where he joined the military officers' school. Like his father, he soon became a leader, in command of thirty soldiers. It was, he says, "my father's will, my father's way. I felt this and I thought, This is the way of the Palestinian people."

With the outbreak of war against Israel in June 1967, Faisal was sent to Lebanon to recruit Palestinians for the army. There, in the mountains near Beirut, he organized a military camp and trained twelve hundred men to fight; but the Israelis' swift victory quickly doused the Arabs' hopes. Once again Faisal was forced to choose between the military and the political. "If I stayed outside, maybe I could reach some high position in the Syrian army, but I felt that I missed Jerusalem, so I decided to come back." Jerusalem was the city of his parents' property—houses, land, and farms—and of his father's dream. Here he could work directly toward a Palestinian state.

Going back to Jerusalem was more than a small challenge. With his Jordanian passport Faisal had no problem traveling to the Hashemite Kingdom, but with all of Jerusalem now in the hands of the Israelis, the only way to enter was to infiltrate illegally. Like thousands of other Palestinians also trying to rejoin friends and families, he drove to the east bank of the Jordan River, found a shallow part of the narrow waterway, and, dressed in regular street clothes, began to wade across.

"Halt!" a voice called out to him in Hebrew, and an Israeli soldier ordered him to go back. Undaunted, Faisal tried to talk his way across, but the soldier was not amused and started shooting between his legs. "The next one will be through your eyes," the soldier said.

Not one to give up, Faisal tried again two hours later, only to meet a similar impasse. The next day he tried again, and the next and the next—until the fifth day, when he succeeded in reaching Jerusalem.

Faisal Husseini walked past the palm trees that lined the main square of Ramallah and thought about his plans for the future. He had come back to look after his family's property, some of which was near this Arab resort town where lovely parks and cool stone villas offered respite from the desert heat. But, with the West Bank and Jerusalem now under Israeli control, he was eager to do more in the struggle for his homeland. As he walked along the square, a car pulled up beside him, and he heard someone call out his name. The car door opened and Faisal was surprised and pleased to see his old friend Yasser Arafat. He climbed in. The guerrilla leader, now making his headquarters in a deserted building in the Casbah of Nablus, often traveled up and down the West Bank, holding meetings in cafes to gather recruits and organize the leadership of Fatah. Arafat welcomed Faisal and asked why he had returned.

"We started talking about the occupation and about the duty to fight against the occupation," recalls Faisal. "I said that for the first time we are facing the Jewish people. We must start political activities. 'It's a good idea,' Arafat told me, 'but I don't think they will let us start.' "

The two men agreed that they must use political methods as well as violent means. "If we found there were problems using political activities, then we decided we could start with military activities," Faisal says.

But Arafat wasn't convinced that Faisal was sincere and dedicated to the cause. "He was thinking, was I talking this way because I believed in political activities, or because I was afraid of military activities?" After much questioning and examination, Faisal was able to convince Arafat that he wasn't afraid.

"You have just finished military school. You can start training our people," Arafat told Faisal and took him to his home.

When they reached the house, Arafat handed him some weapons. "He gave me two machine guns, a Russian Kalashnikov and a Czechoslovakian Samosar," Faisal recalls. "I kept the weapons in my home."

In the three months that followed, Fatah's guerrillas became extremely active, carrying out sixty different operations against civilian Israeli targets—bombing factories, homes, movie theaters, and bus terminals. Surprised at the pace of militant activity, Faisal tried to contact Arafat, wanting to find out if he had given up the political option. When he arrived at Arafat's house near the municipality in Ramallah, he discovered that the Israeli army had been there two days before; but the Fatah leader had already fled the country for Jordan, soon to take up command of the PLO. Says Faisal, "I started feeling that I am under someone's eyes, that someone is watching me." Two days later, as Faisal walked a few blocks from his home in Jerusalem, the police arrived and put him under arrest; when they searched his house they found the machine guns, which he had taken apart and hidden.

The jeep ride to Moscobiya Jail was brutal. With his hands tied behind his back, Faisal was beaten again and again, first in the stomach, then in the chest, then once more in the stomach. "I tried to run away," he remembers. "I was handcuffed to two soldiers, and I jumped from the jeep, taking the two soldiers with me. I even tried to put my leg on the wheels so that they would run over me. It was more like suicide than running away."

Faisal's existence in Jerusalem came as a shock to many Israelis. "It was as if the son of Ho Chi Minh had come to live in New York City," says one Israeli, comparing Abdul Kader to the North Vietnamese revolutionary leader. Faisal's arrest and imprisonment became big news in all the papers. "Jail for son of Abdul Kader al-Husseini," shouted the headlines in Hebrew and English.

Faisal read the headlines from his prison cell and was astonished at the way the Israelis had embellished his career. "They said that I was a colonel, that I was the right hand of Ahmed Shukeiry, the PLO leader, that I was the new commander of the Fatah in the area." Yes, he says, "I was an officer, but I had only one star; I was not the right hand of Ahmed Shukeiry. Nor was I the leader of Fatah in the area. There was no cell; I was alone. And the only thing they found was two old weapons that were in pieces."

His Israeli lawyer, Shmuel Tamir, later a minister of justice, used the headlines as testimony in court, showing that Faisal was arrested not for what he had done, but as revenge against his father. Faisal told the court that he had kept the weapons as a means of maintaining contact with other members of Fatah. His wish, he said, was to convince the others that the only way to achieve peace was through peaceful means. Despite the fact that he had concealed weapons, the court's response was mild: a year in prison and two years' suspended sentence. Like almost every Palestinian who has been in jail, Faisal still remembers the date he was released, October 24, 1968.

After his twelve months in prison, Faisal floundered from one job to another, never really able to find gratifying work. He had not finished university, he had no preparation for the business world, and worse, he had no identity card. "I could not leave the country; I couldn't even move freely in the streets because the police would stop me and ask about my identity card," he recalls. "It was a bad feeling. Whenever I would see a soldier or a policeman or a checkpoint, I would start counting, thinking, Will they stop

me or won't they? Will they know my story or won't
they? Will they arrest me or won't they?" A number
of times, he was taken to Moscobiya Jail and held for
several hours; on a few occasions he was held overnight. Nevertheless, he was treated far better than
most other prisoners; he was still the son of Abdul
Kader al-Husseini.

The struggle to obtain his identity card dragged
on for seven years. As a resident of Jerusalem and
heir to the family legacy, he knew this was the city
where he belonged. In fact, he was even listed as a
resident by the census takers, but had been in prison
when he was supposed to receive his card. As both
he and the Israelis were well aware, a Jerusalem identity card carries special privileges. As a citizen of Jerusalem, now a unified city, he would be entitled to
almost the same judicial process as any Israeli citizen.
He could not be deported, nor could his house be
demolished, nor could he be subjected to the degree
of harsh martial law often applied to Palestinians living in the West Bank. He could publish statements
with almost no censorship. He could organize conferences, political activities, meetings, and demonstrations according to the Israeli law without
submitting to the military government. Even on a
daily basis, his life would be easier. His yellow Israeli
license plates would allow him to travel with less harassment at checkpoints. He could vote in the municipality, he could collect Social Security, and if he
chose to, he could even become an Israeli citizen.
Faisal was determined to obtain the card, and by 1977
he had won the fight; now he could begin a new life.

Faisal Husseini is in the living room of his house in
Wadi Joz, a sunlit, stylish salon with a fine Oriental
rug, capacious white jacquard sofas, and a view overlooking Jerusalem. Once again, he has returned from
prison, and now, in late July 1988, he has resumed
his activities as head of the Arab Studies Society.

Only a few minutes earlier, his sixteen-year-old son had come into the room to say hello. Several weeks before, the boy had spent a few hours in jail; the Israelis had accused him of throwing rocks at soldiers. When he returned, his face was black and blue, his wrists red, and his arm swollen from beating. Faisal, angered by the Israelis' treatment, speaks of his young son with pride. Before his arrest, he says, "I considered him a kid. Now I consider him a man."

Three nights ago, Faisal participated in a public debate with several Israeli politicians, and he is moved to reflect on the meetings he had a year earlier.

The telephone call from Sari Nusseibeh came only a day after Faisal had been released from jail in July 1987. Told about Nusseibeh's preliminary discussions with Moshe Amirav, Faisal was eager to meet with the Israeli politician. When he arrived at Nusseibeh's house at the appointed time a few days later, the men were sitting on the large, shaded veranda. Faisal walked in and shook hands with the others. Despite the fact that the men represented bitter historical opponents, the atmosphere was relaxed. "There was no tension," Faisal recalls.

Amirav presented his points:

—There could be no peace without the Likud and the PLO.

—The Israelis and the Palestinians had been fighting each other for dozens of years, and two items were not negotiable on either side: that Israel was entitled to live within secure and defensible borders in the state it formed in 1948; that the Palestinians could not be asked to abandon their claims to some part of the territory they occupied in 1948.

—Any solution that did not recognize the right of Israel to exist, or the Palestinian people to have their own state, or tried to ignore the PLO would be worthless.

The first meeting ended on an optimistic note.

"Really, I was happy. I thought that at last we found someone to talk with," says Faisal.

Another meeting followed, and Amirav presented a paper that he assured them had been seen by Yitzhak Shamir. The prime minister was eager to follow in the footsteps of Menachem Begin. Just as Begin had made peace with Egypt, he said, Shamir wanted to make peace with the Palestinians.

Amirav conceded that there could be a Palestinian state, but that it would require an evolutionary process to inspire confidence. While a state was not foreclosed, neither was it guaranteed. His position included a set of stages timed over three years and made two stipulations: First, that within that time frame there must be mutual recognition between Israel and the PLO; and second, that the PLO must condemn all use of violence against Israel inside and outside the territories. Meanwhile, the Israelis would cease to expand the settlements.

Accepting these points meant a major concession on Faisal's part. Nevertheless, he accepted the right of Israel to exist in its pre-1967 borders and agreed to the idea of two stages within a three-year interim period. "I didn't agree one hundred percent with what was there, but I understood that I am not talking with another Palestinian, and he understood that he is not talking with an Israeli. So because of this, we began to understand each other more."

Several meetings followed, some of them in Amirav's office, others at the Arab Studies Society. The Israeli brought out a second paper discussing self-determination and listing the specific stages to reach a Palestinian state. There would be direct negotiations between Israel and the PLO (without Jordan) to create a state, but, he insisted, there would be no guarantee of a state.

When Faisal heard this, he was upset. "I told him that the first paper that he showed me said, 'I am inviting you to spend two months in Switzerland; here is the ticket and a bag of clothes.' " But the ticket, says Faisal, showed that there was no direct flight from Jerusalem to Switzerland; instead, he would have to go first to Uganda, and from there take a flight to Switzerland. And in the second paper, Faisal explains, he discovered that the suitcase contained only clothes for Uganda and nothing at all for Switzerland. "If you want me to believe you," he told Amirav, "you must give me the bag and I'll put in the things I need for Switzerland."

Faisal had his list ready: "We reached the issue of the Palestinian identity, and I made it clear we would have our own money, our own coins, our own passport, our own television broadcasting, and our own flag. And the capital of this identity would be in east Jerusalem." He was still willing to accept the idea of a first stage "from one to three years, and then we would reach the second step, which is a Palestinian state."

But Amirav would not agree to these conditions as a first step. "He told me that with coins and flags, with a foreign office and economic offices outside, all the people will understand that this already is a state." The Israeli rejected the idea.

"We must have foreign offices," Faisal told him, "but I don't want an army." What the Palestinian did want was international guarantees through an international conference. "At this stage," recalls Faisal, "we decided to complete the agreement with Arafat."

Rather than arrange for a special meeting with the chairman of the PLO, Faisal suggested that the Israelis travel to Geneva, where Arafat was attending a conference. Amirav suggested that Faisal get permission for a delegation to meet first with Shamir. Said Faisal, "I do not have to get permission from the PLO." But the meeting never took place. On August 24, 1987, under orders of the Israeli government, Faisal Husseini was arrested and put in jail. Israeli officials claimed that he was arrested because his activities with the Arab Studies Society were a threat to national security. But many Palestinians, and Israeli citizens as well, believe his moderate position was a threat to Israeli hardliners who had consistently claimed there was no Palestinian with whom they could negotiate. "Not to speak to them is the height of craziness," says Abba Eban who adds, "To harass these people instead of welcoming them, failing to use them as an intermediary to those to whom we cannot talk, seems to me to be the height of folly."

Shortly after, while Faisal was in prison, Prime Minister Shamir made a trip to Bucharest, where he saw President Ceausescu of Romania; Ceausescu raised the issue of an international conference. Shamir, who has always argued against such a conference because he believes it would impose hostile decisions on Israel, told Ceausescu that the conference was unnecessary. To prove his point, he pulled out the paper showing that his own party member had been holding direct discussions with the PLO. Ceausescu knew about the talks, says Faisal. "He told him that Mr. Arafat was here some days ago and showed him the same paper."

Faisal was released from prison in June 1988 after serving ten months. Although he had every reason to turn bitterly anti-Israeli, Faisal remains moderate in his views. "I can't see any solution but two states," he says. "I love the idea of one state, but it is a dream, my beautiful dream." He pauses for a moment to describe it: "From the river to the sea, to have a Palestinian secular democratic state that Moslems, Christians, and Jews can live in together." But Faisal acknowledges that for now the Israelis would never accept his idea. "Maybe our sons, our grandsons, ours and theirs, will reach a point when they say, 'Why not live together in one state?' If they decide this in a democratic way, then the dream will be there. If not, it will go on being a dream."

Of his debate with the Israelis the previous night in July 1988, Faisal admits he carefully weighed his decision to appear in front of a Jewish audience and had concluded it was better to participate and prove his moderate stance, even if he did not know what the consequences would be. "There has to be mutual recognition by both sides," he told the audience. "The Palestinian side has to recognize the existence of Israel. The Israeli side has to recognize the Palestinian right to self-determination and the right to establish a state on its national soil."

Two days later, Faisal Husseini was arrested and sentenced to six months in prison.

Less than two months after his release from administrative detention, Palestinian activist Faisal Husseini was back in jail last night, and his Arab Studies Society in east Jerusalem was closed down for one year.
—*Jerusalem Post*, AUGUST 1, 1988

THE HOLOCAUST SURVIVOR

Claiming the Land

Daniel Cassuto

"I think that when you believe in something, don't preach it, practice it. I believe, for instance, that any work that you are doing well, with all your heart, is a good work. You can clear the sewage or be a professor. If you do it well, you have—as an individual—the same value."

—DANIEL CASSUTO

Five-year-old Daniel Cassuto did not recognize the thin, tired-looking woman who arrived at his grandparents' home in Jerusalem in 1946. His eight-year-old brother, David, and his ten-year-old sister, Shoshana, hugged the strange woman and kissed her, yelling, "Welcome home, Mommy!" Daniel had no recollection of his mother; he hadn't seen her since the Nazis had taken her from their home in Florence three years before. He looked curiously at the numbers tattooed on her arm; he knew nothing of such

places as Auschwitz, Bergen-Belsen, and Theresien-
stadt. The woman approached him. Her eyes were
kind and her voice was soft, but Danny shied away.
Strangers frightened him.

As the weeks passed, Danny and his mother got
reacquainted. Soon he was no longer scared to be
alone with her. Within a few months, he couldn't
recall a time when her face had been unfamiliar to
him. Danny would sit in Hannah's lap as they looked
at pictures from Florence. The funny black-and-white
photos showed Hannah, young and happy, standing
with David and Shoshana and holding an infant.
Danny was skeptical when his mother told him that
the infant was him.

Hannah Cassuto was happier in Palestine than
she'd been in many years. Increasingly violent clashes
between Jews and Arabs over the fate of the region
raged inside and outside of Jerusalem, but stability
reigned in Grandfather Cassuto's sprawling, Arab-
style house. When Hannah learned of a temporary
opening as a lab technician in the Jewish Hadassah
Hospital, she accepted it gratefully. At first she earned
no wages, but she would be paid if the position became permanent. It was a start.

On April 13, 1948, seven-year-old Danny waved
to his mother as she set off for work. Hannah walked
toward the center of town. The hospital was on
Mount Scopus, in a hotbed of Arab-Jewish violence;
so employees could not travel there alone. They
formed a convoy of ten vehicles—buses, ambulances,
and escort cars—marked with the Red Star of David,
the Jewish equivalent of the Red Cross.

The caravan drove north out of the city, received
security clearance from British police, and headed east
toward Hadassah. Just after nine-thirty A.M., the vehicles entered the Arab neighborhood called Sheikh
Jarrah at the base of Mount Scopus. As they began
the ascent up to the hospital, a bomb went off on the
side of the road, immobilizing four of the vehicles.

Arabs had planted the explosives and hidden in the streets of Sheikh Jarrah, detonating the bomb at the sight of the Jewish convoy. They descended on the stranded vehicles—two buses, an ambulance, and an escort car—and opened heavy automatic fire, puncturing all their tires.

The attack was a retaliation for the recent assault on the Arab village of Dir Yassin, west of Jerusalem. The Irgun, the militant Jewish guerrilla group, had destroyed the entire community; now the Arabs were seeking revenge. The fighting was fierce. Jewish defense units arrived, and more Arab fighters rushed to the scene; violence raged for seven hours as the stranded convoy passengers, including Hadassah director Dr. Haim Yassky, crouched in the vehicles and prayed for their lives.

Not having quelled the violence, British army units left the scene and returned at three o'clock with heavier weapons. They dispersed the Jewish fighters somewhat, and the Arabs closed in on the immobilized convoy with Molotov cocktails and hand grenades; all four vehicles burst into flame. Choking on the thick black smoke, the passengers ran for their lives. One after another, they charged out of the vehicles—straight into the gunfire of Arabs who lay waiting for them. Thirty Jews died that afternoon; Hannah Cassuto and Dr. Haim Yassky were among them. Of sixty people trapped in the convoy, only seven escaped serious injury.

In the house on Gaza Road, the Cassuto children huddled around the radio as the newscaster read a list of the dead. Shoshana wept, but David and Daniel just stared at each other, numb with grief. How could their mother be gone, when she'd only just come back to them?

Jews had to be strong to survive in Italy during World War II. Hannah Cassuto needed extra resilience; her husband, a physician by profession, was the chief rabbi of Florence. Dr. Nathan Cassuto loved his city and had faith in its people. He took Danny and his siblings on countless excursions, teaching them to identify the flowers of the city's gardens and the periods and styles of its beautiful churches. When Mussolini's 1939 racial laws prohibited Nathan from continuing his medical practice, he found another way to save lives. In the places where he had once brought his children to admire the madonnas and crucifixes of Michelangelo and Leonardo da Vinci, Nathan now sought refuge for Jewish boys and girls. He found a priest who opposed the increasingly powerful fascist regime, and together the men created a network of Catholic convents and families willing to give shelter to potential Holocaust victims.

Even as Nathan Cassuto's courage saved many young lives, it endangered his own. The Nazis captured Danny's father in 1943. A few days after his arrest, Hannah received a phone call; she could save her husband if she agreed to come to a specified meeting place. Hannah and her brother-in-law went to the prearranged spot and fell right into a Nazi trap. They were reunited with Nathan, but all three were immediately deported to concentration camps in Poland.

Now Nathan's sister, Hulda, had to be especially strong. She used the network her brother had established to assure safety for his children and that of her own family. The girls went to convents, and the boys were taken in by sympathetic Catholic families. But Hulda could not save Nathan and Hannah's baby girl. Wet nurses were scarce in the war-ravaged streets of Florence, and the six-month-old infant died soon after her mother's deportation.

Two-year-old Danny was much luckier. He lived with a simple working-class couple named Santalini, who spoiled him, played with him, and wished he were their own. "You are our nephew," they told him, as soon as he was old enough to understand. "You live in a little village in the country, but you are staying with us for now." Danny quickly grew to love his new home; as he turned three and then four years old, he had no memories of being rocked to sleep by anyone other than Lina Santalini, or of being tossed into the air by any man other than her husband, Mario.

Aunt Hulda returned to the Santalinis after the liberation in 1945. It was time to reunite the family. Her father-in-law, Danny's grandfather, was a world-renowned biblical commentator and the editor of the Cassuto Bible, which is used in the Israeli school system even today. The scholar was also a loyal Zionist. When he lost his professorship at the University of Rome in 1939 because he was a Jew, Professor Moses David Cassuto accepted a position as head of biblical studies at the Jerusalem University. In 1945 he pulled strings and bent the strict immigration laws of the British mandate until he obtained permission for his daughter-in-law and his grandchildren to come to Palestine. In the land of their forefathers, the remnants of the Cassuto family would be safe.

The Santalinis couldn't bear the thought of losing their precious Daniel; the little boy wanted to stay with them as well. He did not recognize this strange woman who said she was his aunt. And who were these children—his brother, his sister, his cousins? He had not seen them for more than half of his young life.

But Aunt Hulda was determined, and Danny left the Santalinis, who hugged him, kissed him, and promised to visit soon. Danny boarded a ship at the port of Bari and sailed for Palestine with his aunt, cousins, sister, and brother. The huge ocean liner must have fascinated the little boy, but Danny today does not remember anything about the two-week journey. European life during World War II proved too traumatic for his young mind; to this day Danny has no recollection of his life in Florence. His first memories are of Jerusalem, in the comfortable, reassuring home of his grandparents.

It was pleasant living on Gaza Road in Jerusalem, in a neighborhood made up mostly of European Jews who had come to Palestine in the 1930s and 1940s. Danny learned the Torah at Rabbi Efrati's neighborhood school during the Israeli War of Independence; the constant skirmishes and sniper attacks made it impossible to go to public school. By the time the 1949 armistice imposed an uneasy peace in the region, many children had lost relatives—in the Holocaust death camps, in the Arab-Jewish violence, or both. So, despite his mother's recent death, eight-year-old Daniel Cassuto didn't feel particularly unfortunate. There were many like him. Nevertheless, the start of every school year was always difficult. Danny would sit up straight in his seat and wait for the teacher's inevitable question.

"What is your father's name and occupation?"

"His name is Nathan Cassuto," the small boy would say. "He was the head rabbi in Florence."

"And what does he do now?"

"I—I think he is in Russia. I think he was taken prisoner there after the Russians liberated the death camps in 1945."

Danny's fists would clench tightly, as he hoped with all his might that his words were correct. In actuality, he had no memories of Dr. Nathan Cassuto—Danny hadn't seen his father since Nathan was captured by the Gestapo in Florence. But Danny's grandfather had lots of pictures of his only son, and the professor would show them to the little boy and tell him stories. No one had heard from Nathan Cassuto since 1945, but there was also no record of his death. Professor Cassuto would believe that his son was alive until he had information that proved otherwise.

After all, the famous scholar would say, weren't

hundreds of Italian Jews taken prisoner when the
Russians entered the Nazi concentration camps?
Throughout the late 1940s, Italian Jews would come
to Israel from the Soviet Union. They had been captured by the Russian soldiers during the liberation;
because Italy was allied with Hitler, the USSR had
sent Italian Jews to Siberia as prisoners of war. Every
time he heard about one of these Jews coming to
Israel, Moses David Cassuto believed a little more
fervently that his son was alive. He must be in the
Soviet Union, he thought, but unaware that his children had survived, or else he was unable to get out
and find them. Professor Cassuto was an important
man in Israel, and he asked other important people
to help him find his son. When she was Israel's ambassador to the USSR, Golda Meir made special in-
quiries, trying to find out whether Nathan had been
trapped as a prisoner of war.

For a long time Danny shared his grandfather's
faith in Nathan's survival. But the years became decades, and there was still no word from Danny's father.
Slowly, Danny concluded that there was no real hope
that his father was alive. However, Danny's brother,
David, continued to believe. After a chance meeting
with a bank teller named Moshe Halle in 1963, David
was more certain than ever that his father had survived.

At the bank Moshe Halle told David Cassuto a
story. Only a young boy when he was deported to
Auschwitz, Moshe had been a favorite of the Gestapo.
He was allowed to wander around the camps more
freely than most prisoners. On one of his rambles,
Moshe paused in the sick barracks as the patients
received their daily ration of bread. He stood in the
foul-smelling building and watched one patient in particular. The man had injured his leg; if he did not
recover soon, the Nazis would send him to the gas
chambers. They had no use for disabled Jews. But the
patient caught Moshe's eye for a different reason.

While the other prisoners gobbled down their rations immediately—they were all half starved, and if you hoarded your bread you risked losing it to thieves—the man with the battered leg slipped his piece under his mattress. The hours ticked by, and the bread remained hidden under the lumpy, stained pallet. Isn't he hungry? the curious little boy wondered. What will he do with the bread?

As evening fell, the sick man asked Moshe to fetch him a cup of water. Still wondering, the little boy complied. He never forgot what he saw happen next. Amid the filth of the barracks and the futility of the concentration camps, Moshe watched Nathan Cassuto pour the water over his palms and recite the prayer for washing the hands before eating. Surrounded by death and torture, Nathan put his crumpled hat on his head and recited kiddush—sanctification—over the half-moldy hunk of bread. It was Friday evening, and the rabbi of Florence was ushering in the Jewish Sabbath. Nathan ate half of his ration and held the rest out to the stupefied little boy. "Take it," he said. "Take kiddush." It was the first time Moshe had seen a camp inmate remember the Sabbath. The little boy had found a role model in the darkness of Nazi hatred and destruction; from that day on, he never left the rabbi's side.

Sitting in front of the bank in Haifa many years later, Moshe gave Nathan Cassuto's son a new grain of hope. He told David the names of other people who had known Nathan in the death camps, people who might have had more information on the rabbi's fate. Moshe himself had not seen Nathan since the day Auschwitz was evacuated. He thought of him always, however, and was delighted to meet his hero's son.

David's renewed search effort lasted for more than two decades. He contacted the people Moshe had told him about, Holocaust survivors from all over Europe. Bit by bit, he retraced the steps his father had taken in December 1944, when the Nazis drove the prisoners out of the camps in an attempt to flee from the oncoming allied troops.

They called it the death march. Officers of the SS rounded up the hundreds of prisoners who remained in Auschwitz and were still strong enough to walk. The gaunt men and women, with blue numbers tattooed on their forearms and torture embedded in their souls, were forced to keep moving for hours on end. As long as they could put one foot in front of the other, they would live. If they collapsed or fell out of line, they were shot. All of the doctors walked together. Like the rest of the prisoners, they were weak with fatigue and disease, half starved and nearly frozen. Every few kilometers, someone would fall. Then the other prisoners dared not look back. They didn't have to see; the sharp crack of the German rifle told them all they needed to know. After many days, only two doctors remained in the procession—Nathan Cassuto and a man named Stern. Nathan was the stronger of the two, and he forced himself to go on even when his colleague fell back. There was a rifle shot, and Nathan shuddered.

   Dr. Stern was not fatally wounded by the Nazi bullet, however. He recovered, and years later he was contacted by David Cassuto. He was the final person on David's list, the last one who had seen Nathan alive. "Your father was the only physician strong enough to keep going," Dr. Stern told David in 1983. "He was ill and weak, but he found the strength to keep walking." That fortitude may ultimately have been Nathan Cassuto's downfall. All evidence suggests that the rabbi never collapsed, that he continued with the march until its end. The procession ended, David discovered after speaking to Dr. Stern, more than two weeks after Auschwitz had been evacuated. The entourage had reached a small forest in Galicia, but the Allied troops were still close behind. In desperation, the Nazis lined up the remaining prisoners one final time and shot them all dead.

"I believed my father was alive until I met Moshe," David says now. "And I continued to believe until I reached the last of the witnesses, in 1983. Then I went to a rabbi, and told him what I'd learned. And he told me, 'You can say kaddish for your father now. You can mourn his death, if you have this evidence.'

"I tore my garments five years ago, and I decided that for me this is the mourning moment. Now I believe that he will not return any more."

Since then, both Danny and his brother recite the mourner's prayer every year, on the tenth day of the fourth month of the Jewish calendar—the day designated for sanctifying the memories of those whose date of death is unknown. Nevertheless, neither of the brothers, when asked, will flatly say that their father died in the Holocaust. Instead they explain, slowly and with great emotion, that Rabbi Nathan Cassuto was last seen in 1945, just before the Allied victory, and that no one can be certain of his fate.

While his brother attempted to ascertain their father's fate, Danny started a family of his own. He and his wife, Esther, raised five children on Kibbutz Yavneh, where he had moved with his Aunt Hulda and his cousins after his grandfather's death in 1952. When Danny completed his required military service, the kibbutz sent him to the Hebrew University in Jerusalem. He studied genetics; the kibbutz needed experts for its large, successful fowl industry. After the 1967 Arab-Israeli war, he went on to a one-year master's degree program at Purdue University in the United States.

Despite his specialized education, Danny did not restrict himself to the laboratory and the henhouse when he returned to the kibbutz. In accordance with its collective spirit, he worked wherever he was needed. He labored for ten years with a pick and a hoe in the kibbutz gardens; the flowers bloomed, and Danny took pride in his work. Those years were important ones, he explains, because he did his job well. According to Esther, Danny has maintained that attitude throughout his life. "Danny is an artist, he is a scientist, and he is a perfectionist," she says proudly. "It doesn't matter if he makes a cup of coffee or if he solves computer problems—he does everything to the highest degree."

Esther understood Danny's personal philosophy almost as well as she knew the kibbutz ideology. Born in Kibbutz Yavneh in 1945, she grew up when hard labor was at a premium and luxuries were scarce. The kibbutz was founded in 1941 by German refugees; in the early years, residents created homes out of the large wooden crates that the once-wealthy German Jews had used to ship their possessions to Palestine. Although they had been forced to leave most of their capital in Germany, these Zionist pioneers had brought their strong work ethic with them to the kibbutz. Everyone produced; no one shirked his responsibility. As a result, the kibbutz prospered along with the newly born state, until Yavneh was a leader of the religious kibbutz movement.

Danny came to the collective when he was eleven years old. He thrived there; the community became his extended family, with Zionism and Jewish tradition acting as surrogate parents. The hard work and simple life-style agreed with Danny, and he continued to uphold those values even after the kibbutz became financially secure.

Before their wedding, Danny and Esther quarreled about the appropriate attire; Esther wore a traditional white gown and veil, but Danny refused to get dressed up. Finally, they compromised; Danny would wear a new white shirt, clean khaki pants, and instead of his usual sandals, he would put on shoes. But as they stood under the wedding canopy, twenty-year-old

Esther looked down at the ground and her heart sank. Her bridegroom had worn his thick, grimy work socks with his dress shoes. "That was ideology," she laughs now. "Being simple, not being elegant—that was kibbutz."

By the early 1980s, the kibbutz no longer met Danny's tough ideological standards. He was increasingly convinced that the community was succumbing to the erosion of values that he felt was simultaneously affecting most of Israel. "In the past, the kibbutz society influenced the atmosphere outside," he explains. "Now it's started to be vice versa. The atmosphere outside is influencing the kibbutz life." Danny began to disagree with new kibbutz policies; he felt the leaders of the society were no longer primarily concerned with the good of the community. Disappointed and disillusioned, he began to search for a new life-style; he longed to find a place that shared a different goal. "Kibbutz life is very tough in that you give a lot of yourself," he says today. "It pays only if you are convinced deep in your heart that this type of society is a good one. There is no point in giving up many aspects of individual freedom if the society is not better."

It was June 10, 1967, five days into the third Arab-Israeli war since Israel's founding. Twenty-six-year-old Danny Cassuto was patrolling the Gaza Strip. The serious fighting was over for him and his colleagues; they had easily captured Gaza from Egypt on the second day of the war. Even as they monitored the streets for any unrest, the Israeli troops were thinking of their fellow soldiers who were engaged in more difficult fighting elsewhere in the country. The troops kept transistor radios with them in their jeeps and tanks, alert for updates on Israeli progress.

Suddenly, all the vehicles braked to a stop. A hush descended on the otherwise-deserted streets as young privates and battle-worn sergeants alike huddled around the radios, unable to believe their ears. "Listen!" each one shouted to the next. "It's too good to be true!" Pandemonium broke out; the soldiers were crying and laughing, dancing and praying. Israeli troops had captured the Old City of Jerusalem, which had been under Jordanian rule since 1948. The biblical capital of Israel was reunited for the first time since the birth of the modern state. Sitting quietly in an army truck, Danny shed tears of thanksgiving. He thought of his parents and of his grandfather, and of how happy they would have been.

The young soldier remembered another summer day, eleven years before. David was already in the army, and he had brought sixteen-year-old Danny to his base at the Notre Dame monastery in Jerusalem. The brothers stood next to the fence and gazed across the Jordanian border toward the majestic Old City. Danny even managed to glimpse a few stones of the Wailing Wall, the only remnant of the Second Temple. "We were always looking from the wrong side," he says now. "People would go to all kinds of places to see some bit more of the Old City of Jerusalem."

As children, Danny and all his friends memorized a Hebrew acronym that abbreviated a well-known psalm: "Jerusalem, holy city, may you be rebuilt and reestablished speedily in our day." The series of six letters embodied the children's hopes and dreams; they chanted them at home and when they played in the streets. Danny repeated the acronym softly as he sat in Gaza listening to the radio in 1967. Soldiers had reached the Western Wall and were ascending the Temple Mount. The dream that the acronym embodied was finally coming true.

The Six-Day War ended with Israel capturing all of east Jerusalem, Judea, and Samaria, as well as the Gaza Strip, the Sinai Desert, and the Golan Heights. The government annexed east Jerusalem, but the fate of the rest of the territories remained uncertain. Some

Israelis believed that because the newly acquired land was part of Eretz Yisrael Shlayma—the biblical Land of Israel—it should immediately become part of the modern state. While the government hesitated, these ideologues began settling in the largely Arab regions of Judea and Samaria as early as the following September. Household by household, they moved across the Green Line—Israel's 1948 border—and established small Jewish communities among the Palestinian villages and cities.

In the early years, the settlers were spontaneous and unorganized, but after the shock of the 1973 Yom Kippur War, the movement gained tremendous momentum. By invading Israel on the most sacred Jewish holy day, the Arab nations convinced many Israelis that the country needed the security of wider borders. More people began actively to support the idea of Eretz Yisrael Shlayma. These believers united in 1974 in the Gush Emunim settlement movement. The organization's first major success came in April of the following year, when several Gush members moved into an abandoned Jordanian army base in the West Bank, ostensibly to set up a workers' camp called Ofra. They never left, and the camp quickly became a small residential community. At first life was difficult in Ofra; the Israeli Labor government did not approve of the settlement movement and therefore did not help the community establish itself. But once the right-wing Likud came to power in 1977, Ofra's future was assured. Prime Minister Menachem Begin supported the settlement, and funds became available to pave roads, modernize utilities, and build comfortable low-cost housing.

More settlements sprang up during the late 1970s, but Ofra stood out as an ideological fortress and a center for political and organizational activity. Gush Emunim representatives formed Yesha—a council of settlements in Judea, Samaria, and Gaza—in 1979, largely to provide organized opposition to the Camp

David Accords. Yesha is based in Ofra; Israel Harel, an Ofra veteran, has been the council's general secretary since its inception. He is also the founder and editor of a Yesha newspaper published in Ofra, called *Nekuda*.

Memories of the Six-Day War were vivid in Daniel Cassuto's mind as he grew increasingly disappointed with the kibbutz. The areas that Israel acquired in that war, he decided, were important strategically as well as historically. But he knew that many of his countrymen disapproved of the settlement movement and didn't believe Israel had any right to be in the territories at all. Danny was compelled to act on his beliefs. "I felt that if we want to keep this land," he explains, "we have to settle there."

He decided to become a pioneer once more—not in the newly founded Jewish state, but on the western bank of the Jordan River. It was time to act on a new ideology: the pioneering drive of the settlement movement. The ultimate challenge would be to pitch a tent on the rockiest Judean peak, and thus to make a stand for Jewish sovereignty in the region. But what about his family? How could he take them from the comfort and security of the kibbutz to the uncertain wilderness of the Judean Desert? Just as they had on their wedding day twenty years earlier, Esther and Danny compromised. They would move to the West Bank, but only to a settlement that was already well established. Ten-year-old Ofra, they decided, would become their new home.

By that time, the community resembled a small suburb more than a frontier settlement. Fifteen miles north of Jerusalem on the road between Ramallah and Jericho, Ofra boasted row after row of modern houses, separated by well-kept streets and colorful gardens. Today, many residents commute to work in Jerusalem or Tel Aviv, and the days of no electricity or running water are distant memories. Unlike many settlements, Ofra is not surrounded by a fence. While Palestinians claim the community remains unbordered in order to facilitate expansion, Israel Harel insists that a fence is undesirable simply because "we don't want to feel like we are in a siege." Only the bustling army camp next to the settlement's gates belies the aura of small-town security that is generated within the community.

There is no doubt that the pioneering ethic on which Ofra was founded continues to flourish; the community remains the home of the primary figures in the settlement movement. Many of its members have gone beyond the traditional attempts to further Israeli sovereignty by settling in the region. They are part of a Messianic faction of the Gush Emunim that has committed acts of violence both in the name of divine authority and in order to hasten the redemptive process. Flipping through the Ofra telephone book is like leafing through a *Who's Who* directory of these militant Gush Emunim activists. Although these leaders are motivated by their love for Eretz Yisrael, their behavior over the past decade has plunged the nation into a dark period of self-doubt.

Yehuda Etzion is one such activist, a patriot-turned-anarchist who is idolized by some and condemned by others. Yehuda has been an Ofra resident since the settlement's founding, but the Cassutos have never met him. Before the family moved to Ofra, Yehuda Etzion began a seven-year jail sentence for his role in underground attacks on Palestinian leaders and a secret plan to blow up the mosque on the Second Temple Mount. He was convinced that "liberating" the site from Moslem control would pave the way for the building of the Third Temple and, thus, the arrival of the Messiah.

Even as he and some Gush colleagues were devising intricate plans for destroying the Al-Aqsa Mosque that sits on the Temple Mount, Yehuda began engineering another underground plot. A group

of Hebron Palestinians had murdered six young settlers in 1980, as the climax in a series of increasingly
violent Arab-Jewish clashes in the area. Convinced
that the Israeli government was not adequately sup-
pressing Arab violence, Yehuda masterminded a revenge plot. He led a small group in the plan to maim
five prominent leaders in the pro-PLO National Guidance Committee, which allegedly led the 1980 Hebron
attack on the yeshiva students. Yehuda and his co-
horts succeeded in permanently crippling two of the
Palestinians, Nablus mayor Bassam Shaka'a and Ramallah mayor Karim Khalaf.

At his trial, Yehuda expressed no regret for his
role in either plot. He argued that although he may
have broken Israeli laws, he was acting on divine authority. "I saw myself compelled to prepare . . . [the
destruction of] the Moslem hold on the Temple
Mount and, by extension, on all of Eretz Yisrael," he
said, adding, "I was privileged in cutting off the legs
of several murderers [of Israeli youths]."

Yehuda was tried along with twenty-six other men
who were indicted as members of the Jewish underground. The organization was responsible for an attack on students at the Islamic College in Hebron and
an aborted attack on five Arab buses, in addition to
the plots against the Palestinian mayors and the
Temple Mount. The 1984 trial shocked the Israeli
public; while the vast majority of people condemned
the underground, some sympathized with their ideological motives. The judicial process was also af-
fected by the unusual goals of the accused. Although
three of the men were jailed for life, the remainder
received relatively light prison terms. Before announcing the sentences, the judge acknowledged that the
convicted men were motivated largely by "the fervor
of their religious faith," and said that "the transgres-
sions of people like these are not like the crimes committed by others who aim to destroy, kill, annihilate."

Two of Yehuda's coconspirators in the underground movement were also his neighbors in Ofra: Haggai Segal and Yitzhak Novik. Haggai came to the settlement in 1978, after completing his army service. Yitzhak, like Yehuda Etzion, was one of the original Ofra settlers. Both men served three years in jail for their roles in the attack on the mayors. Opinion within Ofra, and Gush Emunim itself, was split regarding the merits of the underground's actions. At first Yesha publicized condemnations of the alleged actions as "unacceptable." This stance came under fire from many Gush activists, and Yesha later gave the members of the underground full political and monetary support.

Danny and Esther came to Ofra in 1985, one year after the members of the Jewish underground were convicted and sentenced. The zeal of Yehuda Etzion, Yitzhak Novik, and Haggai Segal could be felt in the settlement despite the men's absence. The Cassutos immediately sensed the strength of purpose in the community; they say life in Ofra is much more meaningful than life on the kibbutz.

On the surface, their daily lives smack of suburbia. Now a full-time geneticist, Danny travels continually, visiting produce farms and laboratories in different parts of the country. Esther teaches English at Ofra's junior high school three days a week; she plans to take a part-time course on educational administration next year at Tel Aviv University. Two days a week are reserved for looking after the house, she says, and on Shabbat the whole family is together. Saturday nights are strictly fun; Danny and Esther go into Jerusalem for dinner and a movie, or to visit friends and family.

At the same time, life in the West Bank has taught the Cassutos a great deal about political expectations as well as ideology. Initially, they developed polite, even friendly, relations with Palestinians from nearby villages. They would chat—in Hebrew—with the Arabs at the local fruit stands and grocery stores, but the real interaction came with the construction workers from the community of Ein Yabrud who built the Cassutos' house. "Whenever we had to talk business with them, we did it in the house with a nice cup of tea," Esther says. "We also went to their village and we sat in their houses, and we talked together." Every time Danny met the workers in Ein Yabrud, they sent him back with a basket of fresh fruit for Esther. And when the Arabs were working on the house, the Cassutos made sure that they came in for a hot drink before heading home.

But in 1988 Danny and Esther can only describe these relations in the past tense. Since the outbreak of the *intifada*, interaction has virtually ceased. Arab shops are closed; villagers do not enter the settlements, and Jews stay out of the Arab areas. Danny says he is sorry and a little disappointed about the situation, and Esther agrees. "I wish I would know what goes on with them today," she says wistfully. "I would like to go and see them at their village, to find out if they're okay."

At the same time, Danny blames the Palestinians for the ongoing tension and the lack of a viable solution. "It has always happened like this," he says. "The Jewish people were willing to live together, and Arabs didn't want to share. They wanted all of the cake to themselves, and they always lost all of the cake." Danny denies Palestinian claims that settlers are living on illegally confiscated Arab property and insists that the Jews are willing to live peacefully in the midst of Palestinian villages. "We settled on land that was bought—on government land, not on private land. We didn't touch anything that belongs to them, so you cannot say we want to kick them out."

Even as they lament the end of peaceful coexistence with their Arab neighbors, the Cassutos admit that their attitudes have changed after living for three years in this Gush Emunim stronghold. Despite her

initial wariness, Esther has discovered that the pioneer
life-style suits her. Whereas once she was ambivalent
about the territories, she now believes firmly in Eretz
Yisrael Shlayma. And she loves living in Ofra. "I
started a new life since I left the kibbutz—psychologically, intellectually, and emotionally," she exclaims.
Her physical appearance matches the energy of her
words. Tanned and barelegged, wearing a sleeveless
cotton dress, Esther Cassuto looks younger than her
forty-three years. Her husband smiles at her enthusiasm and agrees that her ideas and convictions have
changed. "Now she's ready for life on a really primitive settlement," he says. "She wasn't three years
ago."

Danny's views, too, have changed; he has become
less optimistic about solutions to the conflict, although he is as sure as ever that Judea and Samaria
should be part of the Jewish state. Having lost his
father to Nazi terror and his mother to Arab violence,
Danny is cautious about jeopardizing Israel's security
by decreasing her borders. Strategically, he says, the
West Bank should be annexed by the Israeli government. In addition, his grandfather taught him that the
land is an important part of the Jewish heritage and
legacy. "I consider this land here the land of our forefathers," he says. "And that is something I have to
act on."

Establishing an independent Palestinian state in
the occupied territories is akin to placing a time bomb
in Israel's backyard, according to Danny. The different Palestinian national groups would tear each other
apart, he says, if they formed a state of their own.
"We must keep control," he adds. "I see what happens
in Lebanon—and I don't want to copy it here." In
Danny's opinion, a moderate Arab is one who wants
only one half of the cake at a time, rather than taking
the entire pan all at once. In the interests of national
security, he feels, Israel should keep the serving uten-
sils tightly under wraps.

As the *intifada* continues, however, Danny is starting to modify his expectations of a totally secure Jewish state. In the early months of the Palestinian-Israeli
violence, Danny maintained a strong belief that eventually the two groups would settle their differences
and live together in peace; as the unrest enters its
eighth month, and blind hatred and revenge continue
to rise along with the death tolls, he is no longer sure
that the process is reversible. "Sometimes you get to
the point where you should either give up or compromise," he says.

The time to strike a deal may already have arrived.
His son and three of his daughters are currently in
the military. Danny himself no longer travels without
the nine-millimeter pistol that he bought during the
first weeks of the *intifada*. He has encountered
Palestinian-imposed roadblocks of burning tires several times; on one business trip, Palestinian youths
threw rocks at his car. It has become increasingly
difficult to live a normal life in Judea and Samaria,
and he knows that something must be done.

But even in these dire conditions, the land remains
sacred to Danny. Eretz Yisrael must stay united. Instead of trading territories for peace, the former kib-
butznik suggests, the government could allow Arab
autonomy on a small scale, within the larger realm
of Israeli sovereignty over the state. To Danny, such
a solution would be an Israeli compromise; living with
a Palestinian civil administration in Arab areas would
be difficult, he says, but acceptable. "The situation is
very complicated here," he says. "It is unique. The
solution must also be unique. It should be something
that would be workable, where the quantity of hurt
will be the smallest."

THE LIBERATION
OF THE WOMAN

Mothering the Intifada

Samikha Khalil

FOR THE PALESTINIAN UPRISING 1987–1988

I took a gun and I attacked them
I found myself among vague images
Shaking from fear of the rebel
I hit with one hand and I sprayed gunshots with
*   the other*
An eye for an eye and a tooth for a tooth
Our Koran tells us that the Jihad and the defense
*   of our Motherland*
Is the first commandment in Islam.
                    —SAMIKHA KHALIL, from
                    The Literature of the Intifada

The Palestinians call her "Um Khalil." Spiritual
mother to the poor and wet nurse to the battered
children of the refugee camps, she is a nurturer who
provides the needy with food and the uneducated with
poems and literature. With her ceaseless efforts to

raise money and raise consciousness, she has built an institution and become one.

Samikha Khalil is the president of In'ash el-Usra, "the Society of the Welfare of the Family," an organization with a payroll of over three hundred thousand dollars a year and a production force of nearly five thousand women. It feeds and clothes and comforts thousands of women and youths and, in return, is repaid by their loyalty. Like everything else on the West Bank, the society wears many layers and perhaps the most important is political. Um Khalil, or "Mother Khalil," is leader to the people she takes care of and, as a guiding light of the *intifada*, a wielder of impressive power. She was born to an influential family during the British mandate, in the days when women never worked or even thought of politics. But all that has changed now, she says. "When I was in Gaza everything changed, everything in my life."

The knock on the door was weak, and Samikha answered it almost in disgust. Like so many times before, another pretty Arab woman stood before her, her scrawny body covered in the remnants of a once-attractive dress. "Will you buy my jewels?" the young woman asked, and Samikha shook her head no. "Only thirty dinars," the girl said, showing her a necklace made of colored stones. Again Samikha shook her head. "Twenty dinars—I'll make it twenty dinars," the girl pleaded. But Samikha could not be persuaded. "Please, please!" the girl begged. "Ten dinars and you can have the necklace. I must buy food for my children. They have nothing to eat."

Samikha looked at the woman and wanted to cry. "I too am selling my jewels," she said and closed the door. With a huge sigh she sat down on the hard chair in the space that served as living room, dining room, kitchen, and bedroom for her and her family. How long had it been since she wore jewels? How long since she had had her hair coiffed or could choose among her many dresses for something pretty to wear? How many years had it been since she was the lovely daughter of a wealthy landowner, the man who was for thirty-six years the mayor of Anabta? Was it only eight years ago that her family had chosen such a special husband for her, that she had been the seventeen-year-old bride of a twenty-eight-year-old man of education and learning? How long since they had gone off, starry-eyed, to start their life together in Majdal, a city beside Gaza, where her husband, Samir, would work under the British rulers as the headmaster of a school?

She thought back to the last trip she and Samir had made together in 1948, a family vacation with their three infants, to her husband's home in Tibeh. They had been caught in the war against the Israelis and, afraid to live in Majdal, which was claimed by Israel, had returned to Egyptian-ruled Gaza, where a distant relative had given them a room. There they had remained without work and without clothes or possessions from home while the war went on. They fed their babies with milk bought by selling the jewels of Samikha's girlhood. While the battles raged, Samikha gave birth again. Her family was fortunate, she knew. Almost two hundred thousand Palestinians were now living under trees, in schools, and in tents; and only a few miles away gunfire was taking the lives of others.

When the war was over, and all but the last of Samikha's gold bracelets, necklaces, and rings had been sold, her husband decided to drive the few miles to Majdal to retrieve their belongings from their house. With great sorrow she handed him her last bracelet so that he could rent a truck to set off on the trip. But when Samir reached Majdal, which was now part of Israel, he was not allowed to enter the house. He returned to Gaza empty-handed, with no clothes, no furniture, no pictures, and his wife's last gold bracelet turned to dust.

With the Egyptians in control of Gaza, Samir was once again put in charge of a school, and the family could breathe more easily; but still, life was not good. Samikha had another child, and they moved to larger quarters, where they lived in two rooms. There they took some heavy wooden blocks and built a large bench on which they could sit during the day and on which all seven of them could sleep at night. Samikha scrimped on food for her family and eked out the clothing that they wore, splitting her husband's trousers into two and cutting up her stockings so that she could resew them and give them to her children to wear.

Five years had passed since Samikha had seen her family in Anabta, and she and Samir decided to go back home. They bundled up their children and went down to the rocky Gaza coast, where they hired a fishing boat and two men to row it. For several days the small boat fought against the heavy seas and battled the huge waves. Dizzy and hungry, too nauseated to eat, too scared to speak, the family could only hope in silence that God would see them safely to their destination, Beirut. "Please raise your hand to God," the rowers would say. "Pray that the huge wind that is coming will not destroy the boat." And another time they cried, "Please raise your hand to God to save you. You are in danger. You are near the shore of Israel and maybe they will shoot you." For almost a week they huddled together and prayed, and then they reached Beirut.

As their feet touched the earth, Samikha lowered her body and kissed the ground with her lips. For several minutes she lay prostrate on the soil of Lebanon, thanking God that they had arrived safely. Then they hurried to find a taxi and set off on the rest of their journey. In the tiny world that is the Middle East, they traveled from Beirut to Damascus and from Damascus to Amman and from Amman to Jerusalem and from Jerusalem to Nablus and from Nablus to Anabta, and they did it all in one day.

At Anabta they found Samikha's father, but Samikha was struck by how he had changed: the rich and powerful mayor had become a frail old man. After the family had been together a few days, she found him alone in a room, sitting on a cloth on the hard floor, weeping. "Why are you weeping, Father?" she asked. He told her he was ashamed that he had not even enough money to pay for a party to celebrate her return. "Don't worry," she said and she tried to reassure him that the Egyptian leader would come to the aid of the Palestinians. "Abdel Nasser is a very brave man, and he will return our lands and make us twice as rich as before." Her father laughed and cried at her answer, and to this day she has never forgotten the picture of his smiling, weeping face. After that, she and her husband decided to remain in Anabta, but the memories of Gaza would never fade away.

The Palestinians call her the First Lady of the West Bank, this stern-faced, steadfast woman with her hair pulled tightly back, her strong features bare without cosmetics. Wearing a printed navy shirtdress and smelling of Yves Saint Laurent's Opium, she is sitting in the lobby of her institute, surrounded by scores of women. Well-dressed ladies in silky dresses and high heels stand side by side with toothless women in caftans and open sandals; they have come, every one of them, to pay her homage. At sixty-five, she is their leader and a hero of the uprising, the woman the Israelis accuse of "brainwashing" the youth and of running a major indoctrination center for the *intifada*.

The Society of the Welfare of the Family, which she founded and rules with an iron hand, has been a landmark institution for the Palestinians—a free shelter for their homeless children, a free school for their young, a principal source of employment for the poor, and a free training ground for the uneducated. Its two buildings house five vocational centers, as well as a kindergarten, a day-care center, and an orphanage.

From all around the middle-class town of El Bireh and especially from the squalid refugee camps that line the roads, the women come to her. They come to leave their children in the day-care centers while they go out to work; they come to learn a skill; they come for loans; they come for food; they come for clothes; they come for medical care. In these desperate days of the *intifada*, when the call to strike has taken away their meager incomes and their husbands are often away in jail, they are even more grateful to her for all she gives them. And she asks little in return: to send their children out to hurl some rocks; to stand together in the streets; to hide the fighters and heal the wounded; to shout with fervor the slogans of nationhood; and to bear with pride the flag of Palestine.

For she is, after all, a woman driven by politics: a devout Marxist; the reigning local disciple of the PFLP, a radical wing of the PLO; and the only woman who has served on the prestigious Palestine National Council, the ruling body of the PLO in the West Bank and Gaza. She is so staunch in her views that she has punished her own son for supporting a separate state alongside Israel. She is so influential that, with the decision of the PNC to physically attack three mayors too cooperative with Israel, she sent hundreds of women to scream against them in the streets and to scrawl their names as traitors on the walls of the town.

She is an angry politician who can drown you in a sea of rhetoric against the rich. She is a poet and a writer who fuels the revolution with slogans and ideology. She is an educator who abhors illiteracy, and a teacher who instructs her pupils to put down their pens and take up their swords.

Hit, hit with all your strength
And be determined
Don't ask us the people of the mathematics,
    composition.
Go to your wars and leave us
The time of the political thinking has left us a long
    time ago
And teach us insanity.
        —NIZAR KABANI, FROM *The Literature of the*
                Intifada, edited by SAMIKHA KHALIL

In 1952, when Samikha and her husband decided never to return to Gaza, they set up house in El Bireh, where Samir became an administrator in education. The West Bank was under Jordanian occupation, and the United Nations Relief Works Association was providing much of the food and jobs to the Palestinians living in the canvas huts of the refugee camps that filled the area. "I used to see long lines in front of the UNRWA offices, our people waiting for flour, for butter, or for salt," she says. Angered by the gratuity of the UN, she would ask herself why it was helping to distribute food instead of helping to redistribute the land. "So I started to talk here and there against UNRWA, this United Nations with its many rich countries."

She saw, too, that the countries that had made vast promises to the Palestinians were only sweetening their own dreams. For her people, life was a wretched nightmare lived in the putrid refuse of the camps, without water, food, or electricity, and with only primitive tents to shelter them. "I started to blame the Arab people. They are rich, they have coffers full of money, products, minerals, oil, sources of the rivers, strategic situations. 'They have everything,' I told my friends, 'but these Arabs, they are not doing anything.'"

She had changed from a daughter of the ruling class to a mother of the downtrodden. Her sympathies lay with the poor and her anger was aimed at the rich.

She had replaced the pleasure principles of colonialism with the ideology of the Marxists.

She knew that the Palestinians would have to help themselves, but realized that she was not able to rouse them. First she would have to further her eighth-grade education, a step that few Moslem women dared to take. Determined to finish quickly, she completed the high school curriculum in less than a year and took the graduation exams with her own son. "I passed them," she says, "but his average was better than mine." With her husband and five children still at home, she applied to the university in Beirut and brazenly set off on her own to study Arabic literature, leaving her mother to look after the family. But after two years war broke out in Lebanon, and she was forced to return to El Bireh.

At about this time the name of George Habash was becoming well known in the Middle East. Born in Palestine, Habash studied medicine at the American University in Beirut, moved to Amman, and became a Marxist active in pan-Arab politics. Like Egypt's President Nasser, he sought, at the expense of Israel, a unified Arab nation. While his political organization used any means available to reach its goals, especially terrorism against the Israelis, Habash contributed to his own people by establishing free medical clinics all around the West Bank. His efforts to destroy Israel, coupled with his altruism toward the Palestinians, made him an attractive role model for people like Samikha, who could also create welfare institutes to further their political ideology.

When she returned to El Bireh, Samikha moved forward with her plans, calling on the women of the town to help her. "They were very excited," she recalls. "Their hearts were with these refugees and they wanted to help, but they wanted somebody to tell them how." For five dinars a month she rented a garage and set up shop. A handful of women came to learn embroidery on a borrowed sewing machine.

For ten years the project moved slowly. "But in 1965 we started to jump, not to walk." She put together a membership board of women, borrowed one hundred dinars from the mayor of El Bireh, took over two rooms, and the society hired its first employee for fifteen dollars a month.

Samikha was unstoppable. From the loan of one hundred dinars, she has now increased donations to millions of dollars, coming from as far away as Saudi Arabia and France. From the two rooms the women first rented, they have spread out and now own two massive stone buildings, with a third one planned for the near future. From one sewing machine they have grown to five vocational training centers, from which two hundred girls graduate every year teaching sewing, weaving, embroidery, secretarial skills, and hairdressing. The orphanage now houses 132 girls, and the kindergarten and day-care center teach another 150 children. But the most important part of the society is the production center, which employs 4,800 women from the camps and provides money to encourage the *intifada* while sustaining the families of Palestinian prisoners.

El Bireh is a town with some resemblance to the old American West. Dry and dusty, with one- and two-story buildings along its sullen streets, its only activity on a Saturday afternoon consists of a few youths gathered in one corner and an old farmer sitting on the ground nearby, selling his fruits. Away from the main road, the streets are more rocks and ditches than pavement, and no one has bothered to put up street signs. But a visitor need only ask for In'ash el-Usra, the welfare society, and someone will point the way.

The orphanage building and the vocational center next door are each three stories high and almost a block square. On the facade of the orphanage is a frieze formed in the shape of Palestine, of a woman carrying a child, and the motto "A New Generation for Peace." Inside, the large main lobby is a gathering place for young and old. Chairs line the waiting area, and photos of the latest hairstyles are displayed on the walls. A sign points to a beauty parlor where students and graduates of the training program will wash and set your hair for less than the going price. Beyond the lobby a few girls dressed in jeans and T-shirts are sitting in the cafeteria, sipping Cokes and talking. A few others are helping out in the institutional kitchen, which supplies all the students with one hot meal a day.

The TV lounge upstairs is a gathering spot for the girls, a place to watch *Dynasty*, the *Cosby Show*, and *Cheers*. The large dormitories are lined with beds, each neatly covered with a white cotton spread, but with few signs of personal belongings, no shoes or clothes strewn about, no pictures on the walls. Inside their cupboards, though, the girls have pasted favorite photos of family or movie stars. One teenager, spotting the visitors, laughs and quickly shuts her closet door, embarrassed by the mess inside. Most of the girls are victims of broken homes; their parents are divorced, or one has died, or their father is in prison. But in many cases the parents simply do not have enough money to raise all their children. Here the girls are well looked after, with enough to eat, clean clothes to wear, and once in a while a visit home.

The younger children can slide or climb in the fenced-in playground outdoors where, along one wall, a huge mural shows a panorama of Palestinian life. Next door is the society's second building, more modern than the first and even larger, where the kindergarten classrooms and the day-care center provide learning facilities for children from ages one to six. Here, as everywhere, politics mix with the basics of everyday life, and Palestinian songs and poems are taught along with the ABC's.

In the library six thousand books are available, and the research center publishes books and materials

on Palestinian culture. Here, too, are the large classrooms of the vocational training centers, where
hundreds of young women are taught to earn a living
through secretarial or sewing skills. More important,
these centers produce the profits to provide clothing
and financial aid for Palestinian prisoners and to supply food, education, and jobs to the prisoners' families. For the Israeli government, this is anathema. It
considers these activities a threat and believes that
through them Samikha Khalil is inciting the children
and supplying the *intifada* with emotional fire. More-
over, the Israelis insist that with her work she thwarts
the efforts of the Israeli Defence Forces, softening the
blow of imprisonment and enabling the wives and
children to continue with their everyday lives.

TOWARD FREEDOM

Open fire
Beat our bodies
Our souls will continue to be proud
Kill the men
Put the women in jail
Our souls will continue to be proud
Our death and our imprisonment will realize the
*   freedom*
In stone and in will we will reach freedom
In sound and in death we will reach freedom
By hatchet and by scythe we will build freedom
And in our heroics and our determination we will
*   build freedom.*
—REMA NASSER TERRAZI, FROM *The Literature of*
    the Intifada, EDITED BY SAMIKHA KHALIL

On a scorching day in June 1988, when the arid
town of El Bireh was under curfew, closed off from
the world in punishment for the rock throwing and
fire bombings by its youth, the army came to call on
the welfare society. Several of the orphanage girls
were playing in the fenced-in schoolyard, when sud-

denly the soldiers appeared. Despite the cries of the children and the pleas of the teacher to wait until she opened the gate, the soldiers scaled the wall and entered the building. They headed directly for Samikha's office, broke the heavy glass door, which was locked, and searched the room for books and papers. Grabbing correspondence, files, books, and videotapes, they left the office and sealed most of the building shut, welding the outer doors with iron pickets. The section of the building used for kindergarten classrooms and the day-care center were left open, but the production centers were shut down.

Samikha Khalil was away from her home that Monday afternoon, and when she returned she found her neighbors crowding around her house. "The army is asking for you," they told her. "They have broken into the institute." Anxious to get there quickly, and without a car herself, Samikha quickly found a neighbor who would drive her. Because of the curfew, the roads to the institute were blocked off; not until the car had twisted and turned, first one way and then another, through the narrow, rocky streets of the town did they reach the school and orphanage. Several cars from UNRWA and the Red Cross were waiting in front, there to help the girls who had been frightened, but the soldiers had gone.

Samikha went home to sleep and, the next day, was ordered to appear in court. For four consecutive days she was called before the judge and interrogated, but each time she was released. Then at a little after one A.M. on the following Monday, she was awakened by a loud knock on her door. Alone in her house, she opened the door and found the veranda filled with troops. "We want you to come to the institute," they said, but she refused to ride with them and telephoned a friend to give her a lift. Throwing a robe over her nightclothes, she rode to the institute and found the street out front filled with soldiers. "When I saw them, I said, 'I am sorry for wearing a robe. If I had known that you are all here, I would have taken five minutes more to change into a dress.' "

Told to go to her office, she sat down at her desk and listened while an assistant to General Amram Mitzna, head of the IDF for Judea and Samaria, read the orders to close the society's centers for the next two years. Furious, she screamed hysterically at the soldiers. In the past, she says, "they closed universities, they closed unions, they closed other institutions, but this is the first time they closed a welfare society."

Ra'anaan Gissin, spokesman for the IDF, charges that among the books, papers, and videotapes was strong evidence, says the army spokesman, that the society was inciting "violence in support of the uprising," and that the material contained "classic anti-Semitic indoctrination." One of the books that they found was entitled *The Literature of the Intifada*, a collection of poems and essays by, among others, Samikha Khalil, society board member Rema Nasser Terrazi, and the well-known Syrian poet Nizar Kabani. Um Khalil acknowledges the book's existence and says it was never published; but the army found several bound versions of it—proof, they claim, that it was distributed. One videotape they found showed a fictional scene in which a Jewish teacher, who resembles Hitler, pounds a Palestinian schoolgirl's head on a blackboard, punishing her because she insists "Palestine is Arab" while he is teaching that Israel's borders stretch from the Euphrates to the Nile. The film continues, showing the girl dying in the arms of a hooded Palestinian who assaults the teacher and, with the help of the other students, beats him to death.

Although Samikha admits that the books and papers were all hers, she denies any knowledge of the virulently anti-Jewish videotape. "It is wrong. We didn't have it," she insists. "I am a Moslem. I will put my hand on the Koran and I will say it, it is not from us. This video is false." She denies any teachings against the Jews and says, "We teach our children to love peace. We want Palestine an independent state."

It wasn't that long ago, however, that Samikha Khalil felt differently. Her two sons, both of whom live in Jordan, have had a close affiliation with the Popular Front for the Liberation of Palestine, an extremist group formed by George Habash in 1969. This radical wing of the PLO has sent suicide squads to kill Israeli schoolchildren, hijacked airplanes from El Al, Pan American, TWA, and Swissair, and in 1970 was involved in guerrilla battles against the Jordanian army in a plot to overthrow King Hussein. Because of their involvement in these kinds of political activities, both of her sons have been imprisoned, a stamp of heroism for them and their mother in this society that prides itself on its fighters.

During the period that one of her sons was in prison in Nablus, Um Khalil would make the monthly visit to see him. Since 1948 she had been telling him and anyone who would listen that she wanted all the land that was Israel, the West Bank, and Jordan to be returned to the Palestinians. And then, after five years in jail, her son had said the unthinkable, that the Palestinians should give up the idea of taking over everything and settle for a separate state in the West Bank, side by side with Israel. Across the barbed-wire fence of the prison she recalls him saying, "Oh, Mother, let us have an independent state and put an end to all this. They are taking the lands, they are killing the people, let us have an independent state."

Um Khalil was shocked. "I punished him. I didn't visit him for three months," she says resolutely. When her son sent messages with the other mothers begging her to return, she was adamant and refused to go. "At that time," she says, "I wanted all Palestine." In 1974, when the Palestine National Council, formed by the PLO after the disengagement agreements between Israel and Egypt and Syria, decided it would create a government in any part of Palestine that was liberated, Um Khalil followed the line of the PFLP, calling this decision heresy. The PLO was, in effect, saying it no longer sought all of Israel and would settle for a piece of the pie; the PFLP would not go along with the idea. Like Habash, Samikha was not persuaded. "I was about to get mad," she says. But after a while she became more moderate, accepting the possibility of a Palestinian state without Haifa or Tel Aviv, at least for the present. "I convinced myself that it's all right. I started to change and I changed after 1974. I started to tell everyone it's good to have an independent state." Now, fifteen years later, she declares, "I want to have an independent state by the leadership of the PLO. I want to raise my flag. I want to have my Palestinian identity card." She no longer mentions the unmentionable, her yearning for all of Palestine, and she has even written open letters to Israeli mothers published in Israeli newspapers.

It is a few days after the society has been shut down, and Um Khalil is surrounded by the women who come here every day in a show of solidarity. Sitting proudly like a queen and raising her voice to a shout so that everyone can hear her, she fills their ears with the words that excite them. Again and again she cries, "Really, we want an independent state. We want an independent state, all the Palestinians are saying we want an independent state."

> *I turned the milestone into my slingshot*
> *And the refugee camp into my jungle and into my*
>   *ammunition*
> *And I wrote in blood and blood*
> *And this is the land of the Arabs.*
>   —from *The Literature of the Intifada*,
>   edited BY SAMIKHA KHALIL

THE JORDANIAN LOYALIST

A Family Divided

Yasser Obeid

*Two nations are in thy womb,
And two peoples shall be separated from their
   bowels;
And the one people shall be stronger than the other
   people;
And the elder shall serve the younger.*
—GENESIS 25:19

It was a beautiful late-September evening. Cool
breezes were coming off the Judean Hills and the scent
of jasmin was still in the air as Doctor Yasser Obeid
and his wife, Majdah, drove home from Nablus,
where they had been visiting her parents. Just past the
Al-Amari refugee camp, north of Ramallah, was their
two-story, ten-room house. The iron gates to the
driveway and garden were open as usual; it was too
much trouble when Yasser came home at night to
stop the car, get out, open the gates, drive in, and
then walk back the fifty yards to close them again.

During the hour ride home, Majdah had cradled a cardboard box in her lap that contained the *ma'amul*—small homemade cakes of flour filled with fresh dates and nuts, baked by her mother for the Obeids and their four children. As she got out of the car, she found herself unable to balance the box and open the door at the same time, and the cakes tumbled onto the garage floor. Yasser, who had already started walking toward the house, heard something fall but didn't turn around. It had been a long night. He was tired and wanted a good sleep.

He had walked about two thirds of the way to the back door, through the heavily planted acre of palm, fruit, and eucalyptus trees, when something struck him on the head. Yasser saw a flash of light and was momentarily stunned. "I thought a bomb had hit, so I immediately dropped to the ground." But then he realized that a jagged rock had dropped right in front of him, and he saw a face partly masked in a checkered black-and-white kaffiyeh, hiding behind a eucalyptus tree.

"You dirty coward—to hit me from behind! If you're so brave, face me!" Yasser yelled as he ran after the hooded young man. He caught up with him with surprisingly little trouble and, angrily, began slapping at his head. Just as he landed a blow, he felt something hit him in the back, and a spasm of pain wracked his chest. But he turned and ran after the second assailant. Suddenly Yasser saw blood flowing onto his shoes and he knew he had better get to Ramallah Hospital. Says the physician, "If my wife didn't know how to drive, I'm sure I would have been dead." It took six transfusions to save his life.

The next day, September 29, 1986, the *Jerusalem Post* reported two stories that on the surface seemed unconnected. One was about the stabbing of Obeid; it was only three paragraphs long and was buried on a back page of the paper, under the headline "Jordanian Official In Area Stabbed." The final sentence noted that "as the attackers made no attempt to rob their victim, police believe the stabbing was politically motivated."

On page one, under a much bigger headline that read "Arab City Heads Take Over; Boost For Jordan Connection," was a story reporting that after almost a year of negotiations between Israel, Jordan, and "local leaders," three Arabs had taken over as the mayors of the municipalities of Hebron, Ramallah, and El Bireh. The story didn't mention that Yasser Obeid was thought to be one of the local leaders.

The development was a major achievement for Ephraim Sneh, the chief of the Israeli civil authorities running the West Bank, because military government officials in the three cities could now be withdrawn and replaced by Arabs with close links to Jordan. The article quoted one of the new mayors, Hassan a-Tawil, a wealthy seventy-one-year-old businessman, landowner, and *mukhtar* in El Bireh, noting that the Jordanian government had checked the backgrounds of the three "very thoroughly" to make sure that none of them was a pro-PLO or nationalist activist.

Sneh told the newspaper that the Israeli appointments were "not any kind of an attempt to create an alternative leadership" on the West Bank, but in his heart he knew better: he knew that this would send an important message to Yasser Arafat and his supporters in the West Bank who had masterminded the assassination of Nablus mayor Zaafar al-Masri less than five months earlier. But the PLO hadn't waited for Sneh's message to arrive: it had ordered one of its factions to stab Yasser Obeid as a warning to others to avoid collaborating with His Majesty, King Hussein.

Yasser's life had always been torn by loyalties to three different masters: as a physician, he worked foremost for the Palestinian people of the West Bank, especially the poor; as a Palestinian under occupation, he had learned to speak Hebrew and to deal discreetly with the Israelis; as a former Jordanian subject who owed his prosperity to the generosity of that country, he kept his loyalties to the king.

The Arab Health Center, on the noisy main street of El Bireh, is one of three new outpatient clinics that Yasser has established for the poor. A complete diagnostic center, it enables Palestinians to receive X rays, lab tests, and prescriptions for a fraction of the cost of a private hospital. Rarely do less than three hundred people come through in the course of a day—mostly women in their traditional brown robes and white head cloths. As Yasser ushers his visitors into his office, the clean-cut fifty-two-year-old physician proudly declares, "The salaries of all the employees here are paid by Jordan."

Only a few days earlier he and three other pro-Jordanian Palestinians met with Yitzhak Rabin, the Israeli defense minister. The meeting was one of several sessions that Rabin held in the summer of 1988 to encourage local Palestinians to be more independent of outside forces, particularly of Yasser Arafat's PLO. The defense minister told Israeli newspapers the next day that he hoped such meetings would eventually convince the West Bankers to "assume the leadership in their struggle over their fate."

For Yasser Obeid, however, the meeting was a mixed blessing. He had jumped at the chance to appear on Israeli television and reveal what Rabin had told him: that the American secretary of state, George Shultz, who was about to arrive in the Middle East, was wasting his time. He quoted the Israeli official, explaining that a few months of intensive diplomatic efforts and "hocus-pocus" couldn't make up for the years in which the Reagan administration had ignored the peace process.

The TV appearance was also a chance to look like

a hero to his own people: he championed the *intifada*
to the cameras, predicting it would continue indefi-
nitely because it was supported by all the Palestinians.
Finally, he warned that there was nothing Israel could
do to turn the people in the West Bank against the
uprising.

The next morning, Israeli newspapers carried
front-page stories quoting Obeid, and international
wire services sent similar dispatches throughout the
world. The real tribute to the effectiveness of the
broadcast came in a phone call from General Amram
Mitzna, the Israeli military governor. He warned Yasser that he would be arrested if he gave any more
interviews. Yasser says he told Mitzna, "Kill me if
you don't like what I said. I am telling the truth." As
he went home, he was feeling proud of his contri-
bution to the *intifada*.

But two days later he received a call from an Israeli
radio correspondent. Did he know that *Leaflet Number Fourteen*, providing directions for the next phase
of the *intifada*, had mentioned his name? The Unified
Command had called Yasser Obeid a "collaborator,"
and denounced the three other Palestinians who had
met with Rabin for violating the orders of the underground leadership. The next day, Israeli newspapers reported that the life of one of the four had
already been threatened.

This denunciation by the PLO came as a shock to
Yasser. He knew that two other groups of Palestinians
had recently met with Rabin, and that in the past
many PLO activists, including Zuher el-Rayes, who
helped write the charter for the PLO, had met leading
Israeli policy makers. As far as he knew, the leadership
of the *intifada* had never declared that there was any
policy against such sessions. "The PLO is wrong,"
says the physician confidently. But critics point out
that the other meetings were kept secret and most of
them were held before the *intifada*. They charge that

Yasser was naive; that he let himself be used by the Israelis, who wanted to show the rest of the world that the *intifada* was near an end.

"But I told them it is not," Yasser replies. "What makes more sense than telling Rabin to his face that the *intifada* is not dying down? On the contrary, it is escalating: the strikes are continuing, the merchants are still closing their shops, and the steps Israel thinks are so effective against us are only hurting the people who aren't even involved." But the critics say this meeting was part of the Israeli effort to replace the PLO, helping to create an alternative leadership by promoting the importance of pro-Jordanians like Yasser.

Besides, he says, one doesn't turn down a request from the Israeli defense minister. "You know, he doesn't send us an invitation in the mail. The military governor orders you to come and meet Rabin at four o'clock in the afternoon. You know what will happen if you don't go."

Yasser feels betrayed by his own people, frustrated in his efforts to promote their cause: "I am angry with the leadership of the Palestinian people. I am angry at the *intifada*, its leadership, and the leadership of the PLO. They should think before they act in ways that divide us even more. They should be fair to their own people. They cannot call me a collaborator. They are wrong and I am angry at them."

Yasser isn't very comfortable with the pro-Jordanian label that he carries. "There is nobody here who is pro-Jordanian and anti-Palestinian. Everybody is a Palestinian. I was born here. I came back here from America because I love my country. I love Palestine." But the physician also believes in another vision—that of a united Arab world.

He says, "I am an Arab nationalist," and explains that he doesn't believe Palestine should be independent from the Arab world. "If I had to choose between an independent Palestine or a Palestine connected to

Jordan, I would rather have it connected to Jordan. Why should we create another Arab state? I don't believe in an independent Palestine and I would say this to Yasser Arafat. I would love to see Palestine, Syria, Jordan, and Lebanon unite into a United Arab States with a united Arab passport, a united Arab dinar, and a united Arab market."

In the late 1930s and early 1940s, when Yasser Obeid was growing up in Hebron and Jerusalem, he had everything a Palestinian child could want. His father, Amer, owned the National Bus Company, which had a monopoly on almost all the routes in Palestine, stretching from Jerusalem in the east, to Haifa in the north and Gaza in the south. The Obeids owned six houses in the western sector of Jerusalem; one in Baka-el-Foqa, on the road to Bethlehem; and two in Katamon, the fashionable residential area where only very wealthy Moslem and Christian families could afford to live. He was sent to Bishop Gorbat, a British boarding school run by the Anglican church.

Nothing was too good for Yasser, who consistently was at the top of his class. The increasingly bloody war in Europe, with its advancing Nazi armies, was only a distant echo. His father made sure that Yasser had open credit at the grocery store. He could buy whatever he liked and just initial a small slip of paper. When his father saw how much Yasser loved soccer, he offered him his own team.

At eight years old, he found it difficult to pick a name for the team, but he called it Al-Ittihad, or "United." Yasser was allowed to pick the colors for the uniform, and of course, he chose each of the members of the team. Chartered buses, on loan from his father's company, took the squad from one game to another. Al-Ittihad played against all the best boys' schools in Palestine: the Friends Academy, run by American Quakers; Saint George's, run by the British; Silizian, run by the Italians; and Terre Santa, the Catholic private school. After the games, the whole team was treated to refreshments that Yasser charged to his account at the grocery.

When he wanted to study medicine, after completing his undergraduate work at El-Uma College in Bethlehem, Yasser was awarded a Jordanian government scholarship to the American University in Beirut. It amply covered his tuition, with a generous portion left over for pocket money. Still, his father gave him a matching amount, one thousand Palestinian pounds—a king's ransom then, in the early fifties. Says Yasser, "My father thought that whatever the [Jordanian] government paid was not adequate to what I was used to." During the semester breaks that occurred every two and one-half months, and on occasional weekends, Yasser was also sent a ticket for the flight from Beirut to Jerusalem's Kalandiya Airport.

With his high grades and his father's high income, Yasser had no difficulty entering medical school in the United States. When he returned to Jerusalem in 1966 after three years at Baylor University's Southwestern Medical School, he was stunned by the differences between Dallas, with its oil boom, fast-paced expansion, and fancy cars, and the West Bank, where almost nothing had been done to alleviate the poverty of the refugee camps. The hospitals, like the rest of the West Bank, had been neglected by King Hussein who feared the refugees and favored development of the eastern part of his kingdom. At Ramallah Hospital, where Yasser was the only internist and the deputy director, there was just one surgeon. The hospital had only sixty-two beds for 180,000 people; blood pressure was taken by the pulse; and there was not even an electrocardiograph machine to monitor heart rates.

At Baylor, Yasser had specialized in kidney dialysis, but here there was not a single machine to cleanse kidneys of the poisonous fluids that cause renal failure. He was forced to devise his own method, using ordinary saline solutions, glucose, and a primitive bottle-and-tube arrangement to pierce the patient's abdomen and slowly draw out and recycle the blood.

Says Yasser, "I had to weigh every salt for each liter, dissolve it, sterilize it, and this would take me twelve hours, with my own hands. I had to be there personally to make sure the salts were really sterile and properly dissolved." Then he had to supervise the operation, cutting and reconnecting the tubes and watching while the patient received new infusions of 150 cubic centimeters of blood every ninety minutes to wash the poisons out. The procedure took twenty-four to thirty-six hours.

On June 6, 1967, the day after the war had begun between Israel and Jordan, Yasser was in his hospital office expecting to receive Palestinian casualties from Latrun, an ancient Crusader stronghold halfway between Jerusalem and Tel Aviv. Twenty years earlier, in the 1948 war, the Arab Legion had held the crucial junction, closing the only road by which food and medical supplies might have reached the besieged inhabitants of Jerusalem; Yasser knew there would be fierce fighting there again. But instead of wounded soldiers, other troops arrived; they came in four military vehicles, including two jeeps, all of which flew small blue-and-white flags.

Using a bullhorn, they ordered the staff of the whole hospital into the entrance foyer and commanded them to stand against the wall with their arms over their heads. Yasser pretended not to hear them. Four of the Israeli officers then asked to make the rounds to find out if any of the handful of Jordanian casualties that had arrived still had their weapons. Dr. Issa Salti, the hospital's director and lone surgeon, finally brought the troops to Yasser's office. "You can keep reading," they told Yasser, and one of them, a doctor, introduced himself. "If you need anything for the hospital—food or medical supplies—you can give me a call," he promised.

But the friendliness was quickly dispelled when another of the officers asked Yasser for his car. Yasser was stunned. He had just bought the four-door sedan, a Plymouth Fury, its sweeping rear fins and whitewalls making it unlike almost any other symbol of power in the West Bank. The car was only six weeks old; he had driven it less than 350 miles. "Abu Izhaq," Yasser yelled, calling to one of the male nurses. "Give him the keys of your car!" Yasser could see other doctors peering in at his door, smiling. But no one gave away the secret: the keys were for the ambulance.

A few weeks later, Yasser and his wife had other visitors. Rafael Levy, one of the highest-ranking civilian officials in charge of the newly unified Jerusalem municipality, had come to meet Yasser and his family. Rafael said that his parents had been saved by Yasser's grandfather, Ali, and he wanted to express his thanks. During the 1929 massacre of Jews in Hebron, Ali had hidden Rafael's mother and father in the basement of the Obeid home. After things quieted down, Ismail, Yasser's uncle, had put them in the trunk of his car and driven them to safety in Tel Aviv.

In this new atmosphere, with the Israelis in control of the city and the hospital, Yasser realized that his new camaraderie with the Israelis, and with Levy in particular, could be a big help. What he really wanted for Ramallah Hospital was a dialysis machine. It could cleanse the kidneys in four hours rather than thirty-six; and instead of a surgical procedure to open a patient's abdomen, only a pinprick in the arm was required. But each unit cost seven thousand dollars. The physician initially asked one of his wealthier patients if he would foot the bill for half the cost. Then he approached the mayors of some West Bank towns, mayors who had been appointed by his friends in the

Jordanian government, and asked them to make a donation.

By the spring of 1968, Yasser had collected enough to purchase one dialysis machine. It was the first on either bank of the Jordan River. He also decided that from then on, he would ask each of his patients to raise enough money to cover a fifth of the cost of another machine: "We had about thirty patients, so this way we had six machines within about a year and a half."

But Yasser knew that both Hadassah Hospital on Mount Scopus and Rambam Hospital in Haifa were pioneering new treatments of hemodialysis and, even more important, performing transplants that forever ended the torment of the kidney sufferer. He wrote to Dr. John Sheldon, the dean of Baylor's medical school. Sheldon wrote two letters back: one to Yasser suggesting he contact Dr. Ori Bater, the chief of dialysis at Haifa University; and a second letter to Dr. Bater suggesting he contact Dr. Obeid. The two physicians became friends, at first exchanging visits at their hospitals and then introducing their families to one another in their homes.

Yasser became particularly close to one of Dr. Bater's assistants, Samir Tuma, an Arab physician from Nazareth. Through their friendship, they arranged for Ramallah Hospital to send transplant patients to Rambam Hospital in Haifa. When Rafael Levy heard about the program, he called Yasser and said, "Why should you have to go all the way to Haifa? Hadassah is much closer." Levy persuaded officials of the Israeli Civil Administration to help, and a long-term relationship with Hadassah was established.

Yasser also raised the funds for more dialysis machines for the West Bank. Patients from Nablus and Hebron no longer had to travel to Ramallah: five kidney machines were installed in the hospitals in

Nablus and four in Hebron. The program, under Yasser's direct supervision, became a model for the kind of unofficial tacit cooperation that had a direct impact on the lives of the Palestinians. The dialysis took place in Israeli government hospitals maintained in part by a special Jordanian development budget. Israel, meanwhile, used part of the proceeds from the taxes it collected in the West Bank to pay for the syringes, plastic tubes, prescription medicines, and other equipment associated with the operation.

By 1978 Yasser was on close terms with several of the cabinet members of the Jordanian government; at one time or another he had treated four of them at Ramallah for kidney problems and two were on dialysis. It seemed a natural outgrowth of his own commitment and the Obeid family's links to the Hashemite Kingdom when, in the fall, King Hussein appointed him to be Jordan's chief medical administrator for the West Bank.

The new post was well paid, so much so that Yasser wouldn't discuss his salary from the king's coffers: "I'll tell you what the stipend of my equivalent in Jordan is, about twenty-four hundred dollars a month." Nevertheless, he was still under the thumb of the Israelis: he received a monthly check from them of about four hundred dollars, but also had to report to General Amram Mitzna, the Israeli military governor.

Yasser's budget exceeded $7 million a year, nearly 10 percent of the $70 million that Jordan spent on the salaries of the teachers, mayors, religious-affairs workers, police officers, and other municipal employees. As chief health officer, Yasser was one of the four highest Jordanian officials in the West Bank. He supervised 750 employees: "I could give raises, I could deduct from their salaries, make new appointments, and give scholarships and retirement benefits." And unlike many other Palestinians distrusted by the king, he could travel freely across the bridges to Amman or send patients there to get medical attention.

Yasser's chief preoccupation for the last decade has been a struggle to obtain permission from the Israeli government to build a giant new medical complex for the 140,000 Arab residents of Jerusalem. He has repeatedly been told that another hospital is the last thing the Arabs need: Hadassah, the huge Israeli hospital that has facilities both in the former eastern sector of Mount Scopus and near Ein Kerem in the valley of Mount Herzl, has over one thousand beds, more than enough to care for them; and it is medically one of the most sophisticated hospitals in the world. A fourth of its patients are Arabs, and there are even several West Bank Palestinians on its distinguished roster of physicians.

But for Yasser, the issue was one of ideology as much as medicine. After Israel unified Jerusalem and made it the Israeli capital in 1967, Yasser watched helplessly while clinics and hospices that served the poor had to close because they no longer could get the funds to operate. Inside the walls of the old city, Spafford Hospital, a U.S.-run clinic, closed. The Sheikh Jarrah Hospital, built with Jordanian funds and scheduled to open in October 1967, never did; it was turned into the central police station of Jerusalem. Another hospital in Ramallah was converted into the West Bank headquarters of the Civil Administration, and a children's hospital for infectious diseases was converted into a dormitory for nurses. In all, seven facilities had to shut their doors, resulting in a loss of some 650 beds.

Many other hospitals were allowed to continue operating, but requests to modernize them were often denied. Yasser says the policy in the West Bank was "You can keep the basic minimum infrastructure, but you don't have funds to build any additions." In Jerusalem, the capital, it was a different story: "The policy of closing hospitals there stands on a single, logical, political premise—the annexation of Jerusalem. Once they annexed Jerusalem, they decided they should close all facilities that represented Arab institutions in east Jerusalem," including the headquarters of the Central Health District that stretched from Bethlehem to Jericho and El Bireh. Says Yasser, the policy was "Let the Arabs go to Israeli institutions. You have an Israeli ID card—go to west Jerusalem."

While he concedes that the medical care there is superior to what is available at Arab hospitals, Yasser contends there are other issues: "Here there is an Arab doctor, an Arab nurse, an Arab secretary, and an Arab receptionist who receives you. There you go to someone who speaks Hebrew and you speak Arabic. What are you going to do? You say, I have a pain here, and nobody understands what you are talking about. They have to look for somebody who knows Arabic to translate, and if there is a Jewish patient there, you'll have to wait in line until God knows when. And if you eat something traditionally Arab, well, they look down upon you. People don't feel very comfortable."

But the real reason for Yasser's campaign to win permission to build an "Arab Hadassah" was the poor. These inhabitants of the refugee camps formed the nucleus of support for the PLO and its splinter groups. If Jordan could win the support of these radicals, it would strengthen Hussein's role as a leader of the Palestinians. Through Yasser's efforts, Jordan might gain their trust.

Anyone, Arab or Jew, can cover his medical expenses with health insurance, according to Yasser. But for one reason or another, 70 percent of the Arabs in Jerusalem won't pay the premiums for Israeli insurance; therefore most of them can't afford to go to Hadassah. In Jordan, Yasser explains, "the government hospital is open to anybody, rich or poor, for the equivalent of about five Jordanian dinars [twenty dollars] a day," and the poor are not charged at all.

His aim was to create the same kind of hospital in Jerusalem.

When, in the fall of 1978, Yasser wrote to Health Minister Eliezer Shostak, a member of Israel's Likud coalition, he received a courteous reply. The minister informed Yasser that his proposal to build a new hospital in the capital, totally financed by Arab contributions, required the permission of Teddy Kollek, the mayor of Jerusalem. Yasser followed up with a letter to the mayor, but hardly thought he'd get an answer overnight. He was pleased when Kollek invited him a few weeks later to City Hall to discuss the project. Three hours later, he got another pleasant surprise: "They said, 'You are right, if the Arabs want a hospital of their own, we will support it and we will help you get the licenses you need from other departments.'"

For several weeks, he didn't hear anything more. A month, two months, six months went by without so much as even a phone call. Kollek, too, tried to help, but the answer from the ministry was always the same: there were other priorities that were more urgent. Yasser thought that his initial warm reception had been a ruse: he should have known better than to trust the Israelis.

He had practically given up when, on a spring day in 1981, almost three years after he had submitted his application, his hopes were buoyed. Listening to the news on Israeli radio, he heard a report about ground-breaking ceremonies for a new *kupat cholim*, a large health clinic that Israel's trade unions had agreed to build for the Arabs in east Jerusalem. He heard Shostak, the health minister, apologizing for having turned the former hospital there into the police headquarters. Then Yasser heard him say that for several years he had been considering an application by an unidentified well-to-do Arab who wanted to construct a new hospital in the city.

Yasser's Hebrew wasn't perfect, but he under-

stood what Shostak said then: "If the Arabs want a
hospital of their own, one they want to run by themselves, OK. I hereby announce that today I am giving
permission to Dr. Yasser Obeid to proceed and get
the licenses he needs to build the hospital." Two days
later, Yasser received an official letter informing him
that he was now free to suggest several different sites
for the proposed facility.

He quickly found several wealthy Arabs willing
to sell him the thirty acres he required, but there was
a different Israeli objection to each site he proposed.
After a six-month search, his patience at an end, Yasser finally told Shostak, "Look, I don't know where
I can build. You tell me where and I'll build it. If you
tell me to build it on the moon, that's fine with me!"

Shostak replied, "Now you are talking sense.
We'll tell you where," and after a few more months
of deliberation, the Israelis made a suggestion: twenty-
five acres in Beit Hanina on the outskirts of Jerusalem,
on the border of the West Bank. Most of it was too
rocky to build on, and the only access to it was via
a very narrow, circuitous dirt path. But the Israelis
advised him the area would be the hub of future development for West Bank Arabs. It was November
1983, more than six years after his first meeting with
Kollek.

At the land registry office near City Hall, Yasser
had another surprise in store: "We found there were
over eighty-two owners of this land, and the owners
were scattered from the United Arab Emirates to Kuwait, from New Mexico to Puerto Rico, from New
York to Jordan and Jerusalem." He began approach-
ing the landowners, trying to persuade them to sell
their property so that he could build his hospital.

Three years later he was still traveling. Unwit-
tingly, he was creating his own market, and the prices
of the rocky hilltop were escalating: the same parcel
that had been offered to him in late 1983 for sixty
thousand dollars an acre was now worth two hundred

thousand dollars an acre. In addition, many of the original owners had died, and he had to find their children and grandchildren.

By the late fall of 1986, Yasser had abandoned the project: even with all the money in the world, he couldn't put the package together. So he wrote Kollek that the only option he had left was to persuade the Waqf to donate the property. Yasser had good contacts with the religious body. The Waqf, a Moslem trust fund, owned vast parcels of real estate in the West Bank, which had been deeded to it by Arabs who wanted to prevent their holdings from being dispersed through inheritance or marriage.

The land can never be sold; income generated from it goes into an endowment that can be used only for charitable purposes. What's more, to his advantage, the Waqf was administered by the Jordanian Ministry of Religious Affairs. After several more weeks, Yasser succeeded in persuading the Waqf to donate a twelve-acre site about a mile from the village of Abu Deis on the road to Jericho. The Waqf also agreed to provide $15 million to build the complex.

Yasser wrote back to the mayor, asking whether the building license could be transferred to the new site in Abu Deis. A few months later, he got his reply: in principle there was no problem, but only the Ministry of Health could renew the permit, after which City Hall would act on it. Oh, there was one other minor matter: there was a new minister of health, Shoshana Arbelli Almoslino; she was a member of the Labor government that had taken over from Likud in the rotation arrangement of the coalition. Almoslino responded immediately to Yasser's letter. "Why do the Arabs need a hospital?" she wrote him. "We have enough beds for them in west Jerusalem."

Frustrated, Yasser appealed to Kollek for help. Kollek advised him to approach Almoslino's deputy. Yasser and the deputy met at the annual World Health Organization convention in Geneva. But the Israeli official wasn't very encouraging either, telling Yasser, "You have one of two options: close all the hospitals in east Jerusalem and we'll let you build a brand new one. Or go to west Jerusalem, where there already is a surplus of beds. If you want to close Maccoset, Saint Joseph's, Saint John's, and the Red Crescent hospitals, I'll give you a license tomorrow." Yasser looked at the Israeli incredulously. "You know Augusta Victoria Hospital is Lutheran and owned by the Germans; Saint John's is owned by the British; Saint Joseph's by the French; and the Red Crescent by the Moslems—it would require a worldwide diplomatic effort!" "Well, you have your work cut out for you then," the Israeli replied.

Fortunately for Yasser, the official was replaced three months later and his successor was someone Yasser already knew: Yoram Lass, the dean of medicine at Tel Aviv University. In a speech the dean had given the previous June, Yasser had heard him say that medicine should be a bridge to peace, and Israeli and Arab doctors should work together to build the bridge.

So Yasser wrote him, "I hope you remember your speech. I hope that, as a politician, you still believe in what you said as an academician." A few days later, Lass invited Yasser to his office. He explained that as much as he wanted to, he couldn't approve the hospital. Almoslino had made up her mind on the basis of surveys that showed there was simply no need for another.

But Yasser was still determined to see his project through. He wrote personal letters to Knesset members, former government ministers, and foreign consuls in Jerusalem. He met with Abba Eban, Ezer Weizman, Abdul Wahab Darawshe, and any other legislators who would listen. He also attended the Arab summit in Kuwait in November 1986 and lobbied for funds. Each of the twenty-two ministers of health agreed in principle to donate a million dollars a year and to serve on the hospital's secretariat.

When former American president Jimmy Carter visited the Obeid home for dinner a few weeks later, the project was the chief topic of conversation. Yasser asked Vice President George Bush to intercede when he met him in the spring of 1987 in Jerusalem, and at Bush's advice, he wrote to Secretary of State George Shultz. Later, Shultz raised the issue with Prime Minister Yitzhak Shamir, who reportedly told him, "Yasser Obeid is a very pushy person. We don't believe the Arabs want the hospital. It's only Yasser Obeid who wants it. He wants a whole kingdom for himself."

Yasser had another idea. New national elections were only a few months off. He had been reading about Labor party leader Shimon Peres's efforts to win votes among Israel's seven hundred thousand Arab citizens, in particular his assurance to them that Labor took Arab aspirations to heart. So Yasser wrote one more letter. It concluded, "How can you ask the Arabs to vote for you when your own minister of health has revoked a license for an Arab hospital that was granted by her Likud predecessor?"

The strategy paid off. Nimrod Novik, the director-general of the Foreign Ministry and Peres's key deputy, gave Yasser an immediate appointment: "Ten days later, I got the license." The plan was that the hospital, scheduled to open in 1990, would have 150 beds; it would serve the poor, who would be charged a maximum of twenty dollars a day, and its staff would be paid by the Jordanian Ministry of Health.

These are difficult days for Yasser Obeid. Until the fall of 1988, he could draw on a virtually open line of credit at the Ramallah branch of the Cairo-Amman Bank. Now, to prevent cash from reaching the PLO, Israel had clamped a twelve-hundred-dollar restric-

tion on private transactions. Yasser's movements are
also restricted: he is regularly warned by both the PLO
and the Israelis to stay out of the limelight; recently
his family was forced out of their home and ordered
to lie face down while troops searched the building
for ninety minutes. The reason for the harassment: a
neighbor's child had thrown a stone at a soldier.

But more painful for Yasser was King Hussein's
decision to cut all his ties, to end Jordan's forty-year
claim to sovereignty over the West Bank. Yasser's
position as Jordan's top health official has been elim-
inated. He does not know who will run the hospitals
or who will pay his salary. His dream of an "Arab
Hadassah" will most likely fade away. His privileged
life has been ended by his patron. With more angst
than anger he says, "We had expected that our family
in Jordan would have been more tender with us."

For two decades, his projects were the embodi-
ment of what could be achieved by tacit Israeli-
Jordanian cooperation. But like Israel and Jordan,
Yasser today is witnessing the collapse of the structure
of interdependence and coexistence in the West Bank.
He is squeezed between the heady new mood of PLO
activism and the harshness of Israeli and Jordanian
reprisals, as much a victim of the *intifada* as any
wounded civilian. But most of all, he cannot understand why Jordanians and Palestinians, Arabs who
are the same people and part of the same family, are
no longer working for the same goal. He says plain-
tively, "If two brothers live in the same house and
one decides to build a separate gate, I don't see why
they have to punish each other."

THE ISLAMIC FUNDAMENTALIST

From Moses to Mohammed

Sheikh Bassam Jarrar

Perchance the unbelievers will wish that
They had surrendered:
Leave them to eat, and to take their joy,
And to be bemused by hope; certainly
They will soon know!

—EL-HIJR, THE KORAN

Bassam Jarrar stands before his audience and, with the polish of a practiced performer, shapes it in his hands. With a showman's sense of drama, he darts across the room inside the mosque, a mystical power dressed in all black—his shirt, his trousers, even his curly beard and neatly trimmed mustache, cut a stark silhouette against the sparkling white pillars and freshly painted walls. Leaping up and down to keep his listeners' attention, dazzling the men with his smile, drawing them in with his comforting words, he can feel their pulses quicken, sense their energies flowing toward him. Two hundred men and small boys, shoeless and haunched on the stone floor, sit in silence, captivated by the energy, enthralled with the message of the dashing young sheikh.

For one hundred years, Bassam tells them, Jews have had a presence in the Middle East. For one hundred years they have been building settlements in Palestine. For forty years, he reminds them, Israel has been a state. But never, he says, has Israel had a friend. It has been unable to find assimilation with the Arabs, it has been unable to find acceptance from the Arabs, and now, he reassures his audience, Israel is unable even to find acceptance from its own. He pauses, and rising from the black-and-white wicker chair, he moves a little closer to his audience. Twenty years ago, he says to the credulous crowd, Israel had a population of four million Jews. Today, it has only three and one-quarter million Jews. Therefore—he smiles—the future is not bright for the Jewish state.

There are those in the audience who know that sometimes he exaggerates to make his point. But what does it matter? Bassam reaches the fire in their bellies; he knows how to rouse them to action. The men of the small village of Kubar had invited Sheikh Jarrar to speak following their Friday afternoon prayers. They knew his message was good; they had heard it on the cassettes sold in many shops or in the larger mosques around Ramallah and El Bireh. His reputation as a leader of Hamas, the Islamic Resistance Movement, was spreading. He had been invited to a number of other villages before theirs, and each time several hundred people, mostly young men, would gather to hear him, and were inspired by his words.

Throughout the world, he tells them, Jews know that Israel has been unjust because it has established a state on power alone. The Israelis are in trouble; worldwide, Jews are becoming assimilated, absorbed into other cultures. In Israel, Jews are leaving, more emigrating than immigrating. Israel is so desperate that now it must force the Jews leaving Russia to come to the Zionist state.

In Kubar, as in many other West Bank villages, Islam is becoming more popular. For many years it was ignored, but now Islamic ideas are having an effect. Many in the jeans-clad audience listening so intently believe in the sixth pillar of Islam: jihad, the holy war. With the power of jihad, the young men could destroy the Jewish state and take Palestine for their own. But Sheikh Jarrar never says that; he knows the limits. Many sheikhs have already been arrested or deported for inciting crowds like this one. He knows his talk is sent throughout the village on the loudspeakers atop the minaret. Those who cannot come to the mosque do not have to miss the lesson, but the Jews will hear it too. He also knows that Israeli agents may be in the mosque, among the worshipers.

The world knows that Israel is unjust, he tells them, moving in a little closer to the crowd. It is unjust for Israel to establish itself on power alone. Moslems will not accept such a state imposed by power. Even the Jews know this, he laughs. That's why they are leaving. Peace is what we want, he declares. But Israel does not want peace. It wants a state from the Nile to the Euphrates and wants more Jews to come. Israel does not want peace with the Arabs. Israel wants more land. Its aim is a greater state, and this is a contradiction to peace.

From all around the village they have come to the afternoon prayers, young ones, five, six, seven years old, and elderly ones of sixty or seventy years of age. Some have walked, some have come in cars, some have ridden on horse or on mule to the shining white mosque, so new and pure, with its green dome sparkling like an emerald on the hill. Some of the men are dressed in the traditional white kaffiyehs, but most are young and wear no cloth on their head. Almost all have beards or mustaches, a symbol of strength in the folklore of the Moslem world. They climbed the steps, slipped their feet out of their sandals and shoes, and entered the holy place, eager to hear the words of the well-known sheikh.

Israel is in a crisis, he whispers, bending his body over and leaning in toward the crowd. The leaders of Israel are smart to fear the Arab countries. They know Israel soon will face the Chinese missiles in Saudi Arabia. They know Israel will face even stronger weapons in Syria, weapons that can destroy Jewish homes and kill Jewish civilians in nine minutes. Israel is afraid of the future. His voice grows louder and stronger. Israel is in a quandary. It must have peace, but it doesn't know what to do. Israel is afraid because it knows it will be destroyed when the Islamic leaders control the weapons. We know the answer: Israel must abandon part of the land to the Arabs. If it doesn't, they will have much to fear. The Arab countries are changing. The Islamic awakening is coming. Then, he shouts, Israel will disappear.

The men in the audience nod in agreement. They know the sheikh is right. They know Islam must win. They leave the mosque, and in their hearts they know they must go out and do what they can to help the cause of Islam.

As he leaves the Kubar mosque, and his followers find their shoes on the balcony, Bassam smiles at a seven-year-old, remembering his own childhood and the humiliation he once suffered. He feels proud that today an Islamic revival is under way in Gaza and spreading to the West Bank. He feels justified by the Islamic Jihad movement, and understands why it is so popular among the people of the refugee camps. "There is a natural attraction toward any group that says it will fight against injustice," he explains. Perhaps, he says, that is why the PLO has lost some popularity in Gaza: it has started to abandon the military option.

Islam believes that an idea should have force and be backed by force, and therefore, that force is a right, he says. The religion justifies the use of force against Israelis, even civilians, in the territories. "If he who considers himself a civilian is occupying my house, then he is not a civilian," Bassam says. "Here the civilians, the squatters, carry weapons."

Unlike the PLO, the Islamic Jihad rejects any political accommodation with Israel. Islam was founded by force, Bassam emphasizes, and as he predicted in the mosque only a short while ago, Islam will liberate the country by force.

When Bassam Jarrah was a little boy of twelve growing up in the village of Jenin, he had a dream: he wanted to stand before a grown-up and say what he thought. But there wasn't much opportunity. In school his teachers beat him because he was naughty and fought with other children and played hooky much too often; at home his strong-willed father beat him because he was wild and noisy and didn't do what he was told. But Bassam knew he was lucky, because of all the eleven children in the family, he was the only one his grandmother would protect. Nevertheless the beatings made him shy, too fearful to speak up for himself and tell the adults how he felt.

Every day at lunchtime he would walk from school to his house, and on the way he would pass the city's mosque. No one he knew paid much attention to the mosque or to the muezzin who called the people to prayers. Islam wasn't terribly important to his friends or family; in fact, his parents were not religious at all. His father was a bureaucrat, a customs official for the Jordanian government, whose allegiance was more to the king than to the Koran. Bassam sometimes thought it was easy for his father to beat him because he had learned violence from the ruthless Jordanians who had annexed the West Bank when Bassam was only a year old. His father's family had come to Jenin from the area now called Jordan some four hundred years ago.

The Jarrar family was rich and famous long before
Jenin became known as the place where the Arabs
began their rebellion against the British mandate. Under the Ottoman Empire the Jarrars had been important landowners, among the wealthiest in the area.
Bassam's grandfather once owned a sixth of all the
land in Jenin, about five thousand acres, and was
active in opposing the nationalist movement led by
Haj Amin el-Husseini, the grand mufti of Jerusalem.
Even more important, the Turks were obligated to
Bassam's great grandfather Youssef, a sultan, because
he had led the battle to defeat Napoleon's army when,
after capturing Egypt, it tried to conquer Palestine.
Although the land had long since been divided up,
Bassam proudly carried his family's heritage.

One day, as he passed before the mosque, an odd
feeling inside him brought him to a stop. He had been
thinking about some things he had done a few days
before, how they had gotten him in so much trouble
at school and how angry his father had been, and
suddenly he found himself in tears. He cried for a few
minutes and then, hearing the sound of the muezzin,
he felt that God was calling him personally, sum-
moning him to do good. Without hesitation, he followed the call and climbed the steps to the mosque.

Afterward he kept his visit a secret. But several
days later he had an idea that he thought might help
him become less shy. Bravely, he approached the
muezzin and asked him for a special favor. Would the
old man let him, Bassam, make the call to prayers?
Happily, the muezzin said yes. With his heart pound-
ing and his hands sweating, Bassam climbed the minaret and in his best and loudest voice began the chant
"God is Great." When he was finished, the muezzin
told him that he had done well. Twelve-year-old Bassam Jarrar felt good about himself and knew that he
wanted to follow the path of Islam.

When Bassam was a small boy, his grandmother
had taught him that Islam was the heavenly religion

sent to Mohammed in the seventh century, thousands of years after God spoke to Abraham, and seven hundred years after Christ was crucified and rose to Heaven. Bassam learned that God had waited until Judaism and Christianity had made their earthly beginnings, and that Islam was intended to be the universal paean for mankind. Islam, his grandmother explained, existed on a higher plane because it incorporated the Torah brought by Moses, the Psalms of David, and the Gospel of Jesus.

Like the two other religions, Islam was taught by the prophets. It accepted the teachings of Isaiah, Ezekiel, Joshua, and the others; Mohammed was simply the last of the holy messengers. But Mohammed brought the most important of the revelations, the Koran, which to every good Moslem completed and superseded all earlier texts, including the Old and New Testaments.

Now that he had decided to follow the spirit of Islam, Bassam believed these ideas and felt their meaning in every fiber of his body. He understood that Islam didn't claim to be a new religion, but a body of beliefs, or codes, for living one's daily life. He would have to observe it twenty-four hours a day; if he did, it would help him confront every situation in life, from birth to death.

He would faithfully follow the five pillars of worship. Every Moslem must make the pilgrimage to Mohammed's birthplace in Mecca once in his life. Every Moslem must fast during the ninth month of the Moslem year, called Ramadan, to mark the arrival of the Koran. Every Moslem must pray five times a day, always facing Mecca. Every Moslem must contribute at least 2 percent of his own wealth for the good of the faith. And of course, the Moslem, like the Jew and the Christian, believes in one God, Allah. It was understood that Mohammed was God's prophet.

It was easier now to take the ribbing of his classmates in the sixth grade. Bassam was the only one in the whole school who was religious, and his chums nicknamed him "Sheikh." The teasing forced Bassam to defend his views against his classmates, most of whom were atheists. He sharpened his debating skills and started to study some of the Marxist books his classmates were reading, so that he could compare them with what he gleaned from the Koran.

In his isolation he started reading more books and delved into the history of his people. He learned that King Hussein and his family were traitors to the Palestinian cause. He read that Hussein's grandfather Abdullah had made a deal with the British; he had become the Emir of Transjordan because he promised not to attack the French forces in Syria. The same books told Bassam that Abdullah had secretly initiated contacts with Golda Meir and other Zionist leaders. These meetings paved the way for Jordan to take over most of the land that had been promised by the United Nations to the Palestinian Arabs. Bassam wasn't surprised that Abdullah had been murdered on the steps of Al-Aqsa Mosque: he was a traitor to the Palestinian cause.

By confining the Arab Legion attack to Jerusalem and the neutral enclaves that the UN had allotted to neither Arabs nor Jews, Jordan had abandoned 125,000 acres of Palestine to the Zionists without so much as a fight. Bassam sneered: "Everyone knew this was a pro forma war; not a real war. Besides, what right did he have to rule here? His father came from Saudi Arabia."

Bassam, the rebellious teenager, had nothing but contempt for the king. When the Jordanian national anthem was played during recess, Bassam would refuse to stand at attention and salute the Jordanian flag. When he was told to wear the Jordanian army uniform, he wouldn't; and when he was supposed to practice the smart military drills, patterned after the British-type regiments of the Hashemite army, he refused. The school's principal finally summoned his father and told him Bassam had better stop such behavior, or the school would have to suspend him for good. Yielding, Bassam went along with the training, hating every minute of it.

By the time he finished high school, Bassam knew that he wanted to study Islamic law. But Jordan wasn't encouraging the study of Islam, and his father was furious. You can't get rich as a sheikh, he told him. You can't even make a living. His father explained that to follow in his footsteps and get a well-paying government job, he had to have a diploma from a secular institution. His father wanted Bassam to become a doctor or a lawyer, or get some other kind of "good job."

But Bassam didn't want anything to do with secular law or medicine or the Jordanians. He felt at war with his environment. He didn't know why, and nothing made much sense. He tried to compare the ideas he gleaned from his books with the reality he saw with his own eyes. But that didn't help much either. He read interpretations of the Koran, books on astrology—even the Torah. When he was really depressed, he would lose himself in the paintings of the Impressionists; his favorites were Van Gogh and Gauguin.

At times he wished he'd never walked into the mosque when he was twelve. Then, one day when he was reading the Koran, he had a second revelation: Could it be that he was supposed to be experiencing all this? He knew that jihad was supposed to be at the heart of the universe, that conflict was the essence of all life, but he had never thought about it personally. He had never related it to his own life. Were his squabbles with his father, his disgust for the Jordanians, and his revulsion at the nonbelievers around him part of jihad? Were they natural, even divine?

He wasn't sure, but he knew he had to find out. So he ignored his father's advice and went to Damascus to study Islamic law. When he returned to

Jenin, the Jordanian troops were gone, replaced by the Israelis.

Bassam drove the twenty-five miles from Kubar, down the narrow rocky road from the mosque and back onto the Nablus Highway, past refugee camps enclosed with their forty-foot-high screens, and past jeeps carrying Israeli soldiers crouched behind their tripod-mounted machine guns. He barely noticed the troops driving down the wrong side of the road: "They live in lands that don't belong to them and they want to pretend to be owners."

Along the road to El Bireh the modern and the ancient intertwine. Mercedes cabs rush by, packed with Arab men in their kaffiyehs, while along the road caftaned women carry baskets on their heads. An Israeli turbojet warms its engines on the runway of Kalandiya, the tiny airport of Jerusalem; across the way some donkeys bear the burden of their owners' work. A little farther along, the mosque of El Bireh marks the town of Bassam Jarrar, where six months ago the young sheikh moved with his family. Their brand-new home is a bright, clean place, where the doorbell chimes "Jingle Bells" and the entry room gleams with polished tile. Few cars come down the steep, rocky road that ends at a deep ravine. Beyond it is Mount Tawil, where the Psagot settlement rises at the summit and the square modern homes of the Jews stand above the traditional arched houses of the Arabs.

The rent is sixty dinars ($240) a month for Bassam's spacious home, a fraction of the cost for four-bedroom houses elsewhere in El Bireh. From his veranda, he looks up at the tall antennas the settlers have mounted—beacons to provide early warning of Arab attack—and jokes that his rent is low because his house "is close to the Jews." He says, "It is the last house. It is the end of the road here. There is no road down." He doesn't have to add that there is no road up to the settlement either.

Despite the proximity of the Israelis, Bassam has almost no contact with Jews. His young wife, Gheda, whom he met while he was teaching and she was studying Islamic law, buys fruits and vegetables for her husband and their three children at the open-air markets along the West Bank. The eggs are bought from local farmers, the box of tissue on the coffee table from Palestinians who manufacture them in Nablus. Their electricity is provided by a Jordanian company that has been there since the days of the British mandate. But it isn't easy to avoid reliance on Israel or to ignore the dependence that reliance is intended to bring.

Although he is paid in Jordanian currency and keeps a dinar-only savings account at the Cairo-Amman Bank, the change he receives for his purchases is in Israeli shekels; there are no Jordanian fils in circulation.

The Jarrar family receives some of its water from local wells, but soon the Israelis will provide it all. The gasoline for Bassam's Fiat comes from Haifa (there is no oil on the West Bank); the family's clothes and furniture, including the Pilot color television, are made in Israel. But with the exception of a one-week trip to "see the country," Bassam doesn't cross the Green Line (Israel's border before the Six-Day War).

Nor does he work in Israel, as do tens of thousands of other Palestinians. He is paid by the United Nations and teaches international relations, economics, and Islamic culture at the Ramallah Teachers College, one of seven UNRWA-run institutions on the West Bank.

Like other West Bank Palestinians, Bassam holds a Jordanian passport, but it has been several years since he has traveled to Amman. On his last visit he was met by the Muhabarat, Jordan's secret police,

who greeted him with a twelve-day interrogation and
the confiscation of his passport. Since then more sum-
monses have come in the mail as a result of his lectures
in the mosques and at local universities. But Bassam
has ignored them. "There's no reason to go to Amman
now," he says. "They can arrest me here." He knows
he is under constant watch by the Israelis, and that
they too can arrest him here. "But," he says confidently, "I'm not afraid of anybody, only God. I won't
be imprisoned until it's God's will."

His wife, Gheda, stands shyly a few feet away
from her husband, pleased to see him but properly
showing no signs of affection. She is dressed in a navy
blue djellaba, her hair covered by a *hegab*, the traditional Islamic headdress. Their daughter Hebah,
fourteen months old, is cradled in her arms. Four-
year-old Bara'a is sitting on a small straw mat watching cartoons in the television room; when she and her
six-year-old brother, Amir, hear the sound of their
father's voice, they rush inside to hug him and say
hello.

Not long ago, Amir and his friends blocked the
road near their house with rocks and stones. Israeli
soldiers came to the Jarrars' door and ordered the
Sheikh to pick up the debris. As his son watched,
Bassam removed the rocks but did not say a word.
Though he did not scold or praise his son, he knew
the child would feel his father's shame and would
sense the pain of occupation. As a matter of principle,
Bassam refuses to tell Amir what to do. "I can't tell
him not to do it. He has to learn by himself." His son
will learn just as he did, but Bassam thinks it is easier
today to see the contradictions: "It was difficult
twenty years ago. Now all you have to do is go out
in the street."

Bassam puts the Koran, its leather binding frayed
from use, back in a small bookcase in the dining room
and excuses himself to change his clothes. In his absence Gheda brings a pitcher of fresh lemonade and

a platter of sliced watermelon. Her husband soon returns, looking more comfortable in a tan short-sleeved
shirt and matching pants. Relaxing in a club chair,
he tucks one leg under the other and begins to talk
about the lectures he has given earlier that day.

"Islam is just, even with its enemies," he says with
a smile. "We oppose seizing the rights of others, even
if they are not Moslems." But he argues that the Jewish claim to live here, based on the heritage of two
thousand years ago, is false. The bulk of ancient He-
brews, he says, only became Jews after the end of the
biblical period. "The Jews who are here are not de-
scendants of Moses. They are using the logic of force.
Judaism is a religion. Zionism tried to make it a na-
tionality. We are against Zionism; not Judaism."

There is still a place for those who came before
the Zionist state, he says. Those who were here before
the Balfour Declaration of 1917 are the real Palestinian Jews; they can stay and enjoy the civil rights that
are due to them.

Islam condemns the annihilation of 6 million
Jews, but the Holocaust is not sufficient justification
for the Jews to have a state. "We say Hitler is a crim-
inal," Bassam asserts. "Judaism is not an excuse for
people to persecute Jews." But he points out that Hitler also murdered Christians and other minorities.
"We are not Nazis, but if Jews have a right to a state,
then why shouldn't Hindus and Sikhs and Moslems?"

One point he wants to make clear: There is no
compromise on the central issue. Moslems want an
Islamic republic to replace the state of Israel. "You
cannot ask people why they want this. Moslems want
to live according to the law of God. Moslems cannot
be Moslems unless they live in an Islamic state among
an Islamic society." He sees no sense in talking about
a Palestinian state alongside Israel. Nor does he accept
a democratic, secular state in which Arabs and Jews
would live side by side.

Most importantly, he stresses, Islam wants all

people, Christians and Jews, to be believers: "Islam is a divine law and the divine law must be implemented universally." Of the Jews who don't want to convert, he says, "They have the right to return to where they came from; you know, to Morocco, to Egypt, to Yemen; this is acceptable in Islam."

Asked whether he is glad he chose this work, he smiles and readily nods his head. "You see, Moslems believe they reach satisfactory self-realization only when they are in conflict with evil. I consider my life here as a godsend. My goal is to educate people to reject the influence of Satan. I mean Israel. I am confronting evil firsthand."

THE POLITICIAN

The Risks of Promoting Peace

Hanna Siniora

I think it is a dream
A sweet dream.
To live without the Israelis around is better.
To abandon parts of Palestine,
To construct a better reality.
But Israelis are stuck to their emotions.
And we are stuck to our emotions.
Unfortunately, up till now,
We have only dreams and emotions.

—SAID AL-GHAZALI

When Hanna Siniora, the editor-in-chief of the pro-PLO newspaper *Al Fajr*, stepped out of the shower, wrapped a towel around his stocky frame, and walked to the front door of his house in Beit Hanina, he already knew who had rung the bell.

"You'd better wake up," he said to his wife, "and make some coffee."

Norma Siniora rose slowly from the bed. As usual,

her husband had worked late the night before and she had waited up for him. Now she was still sleepy as she stretched her arms and groaned, "Who's here at seven-thirty in the morning?"

"It's the Shin Bet. They want to take me to the Russian Compound."

Hanna slipped on his glasses, combed his fingers through his silver hair, and dried himself off as he walked from their bedroom in the back of the house. He had known the secret police would arrest him; it was only a matter of time. His announcement the day before, that he would hold a news conference and declare civil disobedience and a boycott on Israeli goods, was bound to provoke the police. Nevertheless, the announcement was necessary. He had to catch up with the fast-moving *intifada*.

The past several weeks had been strange for him. He had been looking forward to coming home to his wife and children after his successful worldwide trip. The Americans and Europeans had praised his idea of Palestinians running for elections in east Jerusalem, and he felt that he had accomplished a great deal, presenting a picture of moderation and flexibility. But by the end of his journey, in January 1988, the *intifada* had begun, and any suggestions that smacked of Arab-Israeli cooperation were looked upon with contempt by the Palestinians. If Hanna wanted to maintain his position as a representative of his people, he had to align himself with their latest tactic. The boycott was the perfect answer.

"Come in," he said in English to the three Israelis. "Sit down and my wife will bring you coffee while I get dressed."

He showed them past the salon with its beige sofas and large credenza. Straight ahead, on the far wall of the room, they could see a painting of Christ and a hammered silver scene of the Last Supper.

He motioned them toward the smaller sitting room on the right. As he flipped on the light switch, the bronze-and-crystal chandelier lit up the elaborate room. Capacious chairs covered in pink-and-gold velour offered seating for eight or nine. One Israeli sat on the matching settee, lit a cigarette, and threw the match into a ceramic snake ashtray. He put his pack of cigarettes on the marble coffee table with its cupid base and looked around. Sheer curtains and velour cornices covered the windows. An embroidered medieval scene hung above the sofa. White-and-gold Buddha lamps, a reminder of Hanna's days in India, sat on cloth-covered tables. In one corner was Hanna's latest prize, the Columbo d'Or, the golden dove, presented to him only months before by Pope John Paul II.

Norma Siniora brought in a tray and the strong smell of Turkish coffee filled the room. Tall and sultry in her djellaba, she had brushed her long black hair away from her face, and even without makeup her features were striking. The telephone rang and she went to answer it. Her dark eyes flashed in anger as she listened for a moment.

"Hello, Kahane."

The Israelis looked up in surprise.

Norma held the earpiece away from her for the men to hear, then slammed down the phone.

For the past twenty-four hours, over and over, she told the police, Kahane's people had been calling.

What do they want? the police asked.

"They say, 'This is not your country. Leave the country or we'll kill you.' "

The three men shrugged as if to say even they couldn't stop the extremist Israelis and their terrorist tactics. But before they could speak, Hanna came in, dressed in a suit and ready to go. This was not his first arrest and he was used to the routine. He said good-bye to his wife and left with the police. As he walked outside, he caught a glimpse of his new car parked in front. He smiled to himself at the irony: he had bought it only months before, after his last car was burned to the ground by a group of Palestinians.

Fifty-one-year-old Hanna Siniora is caught in the vise of Middle East politics, forced to squeeze this way and that. Twice his cars have been burned by Arabs; twice his office has been attacked by Jews. He has been praised by the Israelis and punished by the Palestinians, complimented by his colleagues and castigated too, as he maneuvers between his own ideas and those of the PLO. Some Arabs see him as farsighted; others believe he is blind. Some Israeli leaders cheer him for his courage; others call for his arrest.

"I don't please the radicals on the Israeli side; I don't please the radicals on the Palestinian side. But my conscience is clear," he says. "I am happy with what I have been doing."

What he has been doing is trying to work out a moderate solution for a Palestinian state. He has dared to sign documents with Israeli leaders; he has presented a position paper to the American secretary of state; and he has advanced the idea of an Arab slate for Jerusalem elections. He speaks out boldly in a quiet voice: sometimes his words are accepted; mostly they fall on deaf ears. To the Palestinians he offers hope at a time when there is little. To the Israelis he offers gentle steps to smooth a painful change.

Hanna Siniora drove up to the door of the King David Hotel and walked inside. It was a strange feeling to be in the hotel where few Arabs had stayed since the British mandate. He remembered how, as a child, he had heard his parents' stories of the elegant hotel and how Arab kings and sheikhs sat in the exotic lobby with its Levantine motifs, sipping tea served by black-skinned waiters in white gloves and white djellabas, red sashes slung across their chests, red fezzes on their heads. Now he stepped into the same lobby and gazed about him. The blue-and-gold Egyptian-inspired ceilings and walls seemed to resonate with history. Before him had walked some of the world's greatest peacemakers: Henry Kissinger; American presidents Carter, Ford, and Nixon; and Winston Churchill. Ten years earlier, Anwar Sadat had broken the long absence of Arab guests and had spent three nights in the hotel on his historic visit to Jerusalem. Ironically, it was the Israeli leader with whom Sadat signed the peace agreement who had destroyed an entire wing of the hotel forty years before. Menachem Begin had been a member of the infamous Irgun, the underground terrorist group that had blown up part of the hotel, killing ninety-one civilians, including British, Arabs, and Jews. But even Begin had changed enough in his lifetime to sign an agreement with the leader of the largest country in the Arab world. Anwar Sadat had made peace with the Israelis. Hanna had no pretensions to being another Sadat; but maybe the work he was about to do could help just a little to create independence for his own people.

He walked down the hall toward the sign that said "Oak Room." Pushing open the door, he drew in his breath. "Welcome," said the familiar voice in the measured British accent. Abba Eban, the distinguished diplomat and Labor party leader, extended his arm and shook hands with Hanna. There were others in the room too: Elias Freij, the Christian mayor of Bethlehem; Basil and Said Kanaan, businessmen from Nablus; and several Israelis from the Knesset shook hands with him and said hello. As they all sat down at the long conference table, Hanna took in the scene. The dark, oak-paneled room was elegant, lighted by a pewter chandelier and graced with floral vases. What a marvelous place for him and Abba Eban to write their own declaration of understanding.

The men had worked together previously. This meeting, they all knew, was only for the formalities. Still, they had to look over the papers that had been prepared earlier. Hanna nodded in agreement as he read that the basis of the statement was mutual recognition and mutual self-determination. They concurred that negotiations for a peaceful solution could come about only through an international conference and that each side would choose its own representatives. To Hanna the statement was not outrageous. In fact, he had received a quiet nod of approval from the PLO before he went ahead. Still, he was nervous as he read the words that would show there could be understanding between two long-standing enemies. He had no idea how the public would react. He didn't have to wait long to find out.

The next day, March 26, 1987, the newspapers carried the story of the document and Hanna's phone was ringing nonstop. One after another, his friends called to congratulate him; but three men who should have called did not. Sari Nusseibeh, professor at Bir Zeit; Faisal Husseini, head of the Arab Studies Society; and Radwan Abu Ayash, president of the Arab Journalists' Association, all rejected the statement, saying that it should have explicitly mentioned the PLO. Hanna insisted that the PLO had been included implicitly. Besides, the Israelis were not about to sign overtly with the PLO. And the Palestinians needed to begin talking to the Israelis. Abba Eban had even announced, "This was the first time Israelis and Palestinians have signed anything together."

That night, as Hanna got into bed, he felt good about what he had done. At least he had taken a first step. He fell into a deep sleep and was annoyed when his wife tried to wake him.

"Hanna, get up!" she cried.

"What's the matter?" he mumbled.

"I can smell smoke. I think the car's on fire."

Hanna rushed to the front window with Norma just behind him. He could see his Peugeot completely ablaze and her Ford just starting to burn. He hurried to the phone to call the police, and the man at the other end guessed at once what had happened. Hanna's statement had infuriated the militant wings of the PLO, who wanted an armed struggle. The radicals had sent him a message.

But Hanna was not about to be stopped. The only solution he could envision was a peaceful one. The only way to accomplish it was to act accordingly.

For several months after he signed the paper with Abba Eban, Hanna thought about some ideas expressed by Sari Nusseibeh. The Bir Zeit professor had suggested that, despite their dreams of a separate Arab state, the Palestinians were falling more and more into the real world of the Israelis. The occupation had made them dependent, and consciously or not, the Israelization of the Arabs was taking place. West Bank Palestinians had become part of the system, "doing everything, from buying trousers to selling kippers in the Old City, to working on the construction of settlements. Ninety percent of what we consume," Nusseibeh had said, "is Israeli made." The only way out was to play the game even better. If the Palestinians took advantage of the demographics, eventually they would control the country. The birth rate of the Arabs was twice that of the Jews: in fifty years they would be the majority of a secular democratic state.

As a citizen of east Jerusalem, Hanna could start the process moving. Although the national elections were closed to them, Arabs in the unified city were allowed, and even encouraged, to participate in the municipal vote. In the past the Palestinians had considered voting as a form of collaboration; few Arabs in east Jerusalem would take part. But now, as Hanna reconsidered his friend's theories, they began to make more sense. Why not run for city council and use that as a base from which to call for Jerusalem as a city of dual sovereignty, "open and undivided"—capital of Israel and capital of a Palestinian state?

Hanna's strategy was to use Israel's democratic system and infiltrate local politics, establishing a foothold from within. With the Arabs representing over

25 percent of the city's total population, the Palestinians could at the very least become power brokers in the city council. Furthermore, with the Arab population in the occupied territories growing at a far greater rate than the overall Jewish population in Israel, eventually the Palestinians could have a controlling bloc in the Knesset. Hanna saw it as an opportunity to call for Palestinians' national rights.

On June 5, 1987, Hanna met with a group of foreign journalists and announced his idea. The reaction was immediate. West Bank Palestinians, like Bassam Shakaa, the former mayor of Nablus, said such a decision could never be seen as respectable in Palestinians' eyes. Even Sari Nusseibeh told the press that Hanna's proposal had come too early and was a tactic to be "brandished" rather than used. Liberal Israeli leaders, like Mayor Teddy Kollek, applauded the idea, but other members of the right-wing Likud accused Hanna of being an emissary of Arafat and announced he should be barred from running. Once again Palestinian radicals reacted with violence, burning his car and blackening his name in hateful graffiti on east Jerusalem walls.

"I feel we have in our area only two alternatives," says Hanna Siniora now, "either to coexist and live together or to commit mutual national suicide. I prefer the first option." For Hanna the words have special meaning: the life of his own child was saved by the Israelis.

Three-year-old Simon Siniora had been running a high fever for several days, crying to his mother that his back hurt. Norma had taken him to the family doctor, but the medicine had done no good. On the doctor's instructions she had put her son in the bathtub to cool him down and when she did, she noticed pus coming from a birthmark on his back. Frantic because the fever was still rising, she took Simon to the nearby hospital the next day. She mentioned the birthmark, but no one paid much attention. The Arab doctors at Makassed diagnosed the illness as meningitis and treated Simon with antibiotics; the fever went down for a while, but as the medicine was withdrawn the fever came back again. Once more they gave him the medicine; once more the fever went down. Once more they stopped the medicine, and once more the fever returned.

For nearly a month Simon lay in his hospital bed while the doctors tried to find a cure. During the days, his mother would stay with him. During the night, Hanna would come. But his parents could only watch in anguish as their little boy grew worse. Finally, the doctors tried treating him with cortisone, but even that did not work. In fact, Simon became even more feverish, as well as bloated from the cortisone, but the doctors had run out of ideas.

Norma was desperate. A pharmacist she knew had a friend at Hadassah Hospital. "Why don't you take him there?" he asked. Norma thought for a minute and decided the man was right. Hanna objected to the Jewish hospital, but his wife did not care. "I'm taking him to Hadassah," she announced.

For the first few days at Hadassah, the neurosurgeons analyzed the disease. They immediately studied the birthmark, X-rayed the boy's spine with special machines, and diagnosed the problem as a fistula in his spinal cord. The effects of the brain disease could be retardation, deafness, even death. The only way to treat it was with antibiotics directly to the brain and an operation on his spine. But the operation would take seven hours, and even with that, something could go wrong. The spine was such a sensitive part of the body, if something slipped, or if some of the nerves were damaged, Simon would be paralyzed, never again able to walk. "It's a chance we have to take," they said, "if you want him to stay alive."

The parents told the doctors to go ahead with the surgery. For seven and one-half hours the next day

Hanna and Norma paced the waiting room. Would
Simon live? Would he be retarded? Would he walk?
Finally, looking pale and drawn, the weary surgeon
came in. "Everything is okay," he said. "He can move
his legs." Tears of joy and relief filled their eyes as
they heard the doctor's words. Their son would be
all right. Christmas came a few days later and Simon
celebrated in the Jewish hospital. Only one week after
that they were able to bring their little boy home. Says
Hanna, "Only with the help of some very experienced
Jewish doctors was his life saved."

"If the Israelis used some of the gifts they possess,
some of the skills that they know how to use, like
health care, it would be a goodwill ambassador not
only to the Palestinians but to the Arab world."
Hanna is in his office at *Al Fajr*, in a small stone
building in the eastern part of Jerusalem. Across the
front door is a heavy wire mesh—protection against
the hand grenades that have been thrown in the past.

Inside, the rooms are small and the bare office is
as much a political statement as it is a journalist's
work space. A map of Israel, Gaza, and the West Bank
is on one wall; dated 1934, but printed only three
years ago by the Arab Studies Society, it shows no
Israeli cities, no Jewish towns. From the Mediterranean Sea in the west to the Jordan River in the east,
from the Lebanese-Syrian border in the north to Egypt
and the Gulf of Aqaba in the south, all is marked in
Arabic and all is labeled Palestine. It was done, he
says, to show the Arab villages that have been
destroyed.

On another wall hangs a painting of leaves and
thorns, the triangular green stamp of the censor in the
center. The picture, a protest against Israeli censorship
of the Arab press, is by one of *Al Fajr's* artists, painted
when the paper was shut down for a month.

On the one hand Hanna speaks of the Israelis'
strengths, of their sophisticated systems for health and

education; but on the other, he berates their military occupation and their strict control of the press.

"The Israeli people have the possibility to reach out and become a really needed and esteemed part of the Middle East through education and health," he says. One of his own goals is to gain better hospital facilities for the Palestinians and to encourage Israeli medical experts to train Palestinian doctors "to reach the same level of proficiency." Shaking his head, he says sadly that the Israelis' budget for the occupied territories reflects their primary concern for security; little is left over for the welfare of the Palestinians. What's worse, rather than expressing their humanistic side, the Israelis "are trying to intimidate the region through their strength." But he notes, "Strength in our area is relative. All you have to do is study how many empires came and went."

Hanna believes that Israel's intimidation is not only military but economic as well. He cites the research of Meron Benvenisti, an Israeli who runs the West Bank Data Project, and claims that Israel collects a surplus of $100 million every year from Palestinian taxation. What is more, "the occupied territories have become both a cheap labor pool for Israeli factories and services and, at the same time, a dumping ground for Israeli goods. The occupied territories are a billion-dollar market for the State of Israel, and one which is next door. It is the second-biggest market after the United States."

But Hanna argues that if the West Bank and Gaza were independent, they could become an even greater source of Israeli income. In an era of peace, the Israelis could have extended markets, selling goods and services not just to the one and one-half million Palestinians but to the 200 million people in the Arab world. Today, he says, Israel, Jordan, and the occupied territories are all dependent on foreign aid. "With peace and stability, prosperity comes."

As Hanna speaks, reporters come in and out, putting freshly written copy on his desk and picking up censored stories in disgust. Shirt collar open, sleeves rolled up, Hanna begins to look at the Arabic pages that have just come back from the Israeli censors, a procedure that persists every day from ten in the morning until midnight. *Al Fajr* publishes an Arabic edition daily, seven times a week, with a circulation of twenty thousand and an actual readership, Hanna says, of many times that amount. "Because of the bad economic conditions, every issue has about ten readers." *Al Fajr*'s English edition, published weekly, has a circulation of ten thousand. The paper in English has "equal rights, like the Israeli papers," he explains, and the censor's requirements are not severe, limited only to security matters. But unlike the Israeli papers, its distribution is limited. Because the English edition is only lightly censored and could incite the Palestinians, "it's legal in Jerusalem, it's legal in Israel, but it's illegal in the West Bank and Gaza Strip."

The Arabic edition, however, is sold in the occupied territories. Although it is easy to distribute in the West Bank, sending it to Gaza requires an export license from Jerusalem and an import license from Gaza. There are also tighter restrictions for the Arabic paper. "We have to send every single thing we publish: even the death notices, even the crossword puzzle, even the sports page, even the ads. Because," he explains, "sometimes an innocent news item in our eyes doesn't look innocent in the Israeli eyes and we pay a heavy price—closing the paper or stopping the distribution."

Most of the local news stories are taken from other news organizations, usually from Israeli radio and the Hebrew press, sometimes from the Arab media. But although almost everything has been published already in Israel, "even with that we are not allowed to publish it," Hanna complains. "We took one picture from an Israeli paper and we reprinted it.

We had our paper closed for ten days." The picture showed a Palestinian being beaten during a demonstration.

Hanna turns to a story that originated in the Hebrew paper *Ma'ariv* in February 1988; it tells how Israeli soldiers had bulldozed a ditch, ordered three or four Palestinians to lie down in it, and then shoveled dirt over them. *Al Fajr* had taken the story from *Ma'ariv* and translated it into Arabic. Although the incident, which created a sensation, was allowed to run in Hebrew and English papers, it was not permitted to be published in Arabic, presumably because it would incite the public to riot.

On another occasion, *Al Fajr* ran a small piece announcing that the mayor of Nablus was mourning three Palestinians who had died. "It was just a death notice, and it was taken out," he says. "They don't give a reason. They say it's according to emergency regulations."

Israeli law also requires that newspapers have no blank spaces. That, of course, would indicate censorship; so the editor is obliged to plug the holes with anything he can find. By the time the last stories come back from the censor, around midnight, the staff must look for advertisements just to fill the empty spots. Says Hanna, "We publish free advertisements because we can't have blank space." The paper is then printed at three A.M. and out on the newsstands by five that morning.

Al Fajr was started by Hanna's cousin Youssef Nasser in 1972. The paper was strongly against the Jordanian influence and just as strongly opposed to the Israeli occupation. But Nasser paid a price for his independence: two years later he was kidnapped by pro-Jordanian Palestinians and presumed murdered, but his body was never found. "They thought by kidnapping him both sides will shut him up and the paper will fall." Hanna, who had been working as a phar-

macist in his family's business, was asked to take over
the paper until Nasser returned. "My temporary work
continued from '74 until today," he says.

The years have not gone so smoothly. In 1982
and 1983 the paper's front door was blown up and
the offices themselves were fire-bombed. Two years
later the offices were smashed and the computers destroyed. Hanna says that Israeli extremists confessed
to the crimes. More harassment has come from the
Israeli government: several members of the staff have
been imprisoned, and Hanna has been interrogated
seven times.

Despite the hostility and destruction from some
Israelis, Hanna has been able to use the paper for
constructive purposes. In his position as editor, he is
an influential representative of the people and an important supporter of the PLO, able to present his ideas
for peace. Six months of the year he travels around
the world, pursuing patronage for the Palestinians at
home. In Jerusalem, Hanna Siniora receives foreign
ministers as if he were a head of state.

The American Colony Hotel is an oasis of quiet in
east Jerusalem, its only noises the gentle running of
a fountain and the sweet chirpings of the birds. Once
the fabulous home of a Turkish pasha, it is now the
center of elite Palestinian life. Foreign journalists and
PLO supporters convene in its palm-treed courtyard,
exchanging stories over Turkish coffee and mint iced
tea. The Israelis call the American Colony "the press-
room of the PLO." Influential visitors call it home.

When dignitaries and foreign ministers come to
see Israeli officials in the capital, they often stop here
to meet with the Palestinian side. Such was the case
when the American secretary of state, George Shultz,
came to Jerusalem in February 1988. Shultz had already met with Hanna Siniora and Fayez Abu Rahme,
head of the Gaza Lawyers' Association, in Washington, D.C., the month before. The two Palestinians had

presented a fourteen-point paper. Among the items it called for were an international conference as a forum for negotiations between Israel and her Arab adversaries. The paper also emphasized the aspirations of the Palestinians: their "national rights of self-determination" and "the establishment of an independent state on our national soil under the leadership of the PLO as our sole legitimate representative." George Shultz, a strong supporter of Israel, nonetheless assured the men he would try to help. Hanna felt heartened. "Even the Executive Committee of the PLO appreciated our efforts and said so publicly in the Arab press."

The following month Shultz arrived in Jerusalem with a peace plan he had worked out; it accepted the international conference, but only as an umbrella for starting direct peace talks. When Shultz brought his idea to the Israeli prime minister, Yitzhak Shamir, Shamir all but rejected it, refusing to accept the international conference. Undaunted, Shultz continued, going next to the American Colony to see Siniora, Abu Rahme, and other Palestinians. But no one was there to greet him. The PLO had sent orders from its headquarters in Tunis that no Palestinian delegation could see the American unless the group included PLO supporters from outside the occupied territories. Hanna Siniora had been thwarted by the leaders of the PLO.

It is May 1988, five months after the start of the uprising, and Hanna Siniora has been invited to speak at an Arab convention near Washington, D.C. When he mounts the podium dressed in a navy blue suit, white-striped shirt, and navy-striped tie, his stocky frame and broad, mustached face dominate the dais. But his style is more subdued than sensational, and his monotone delivery disguises his passions. He speaks slowly in a quiet voice; a master of modesty, skilled at restraint.

"My presence is a tribute to the people who are

conducting the uprising," he says to much applause, "because through their efforts Palestinians and Arabs have regained their dignity, their pride, their assurance." And, he emphasizes, his presence is especially a tribute "to the Palestinians under occupation," because they have "regained their pride by relying on their own efforts."

For the past three years Siniora has been delivering speeches like this one to groups around the world, from the U.S. and Europe to Africa and Australia, but it is only in the last five months that he has been able to talk about the self-reliance of the Palestinians. With the uprising has come a sense of freedom and greater self-esteem; through it they have discovered their ability to fight their own battle without relying on the rest of the Arab world. Ironically, it is because of the failure of the other Arabs to help them politically, militarily, or economically that the Palestinians under occupation have finally taken matters into their own hands. In fact, Siniora implies, all Arabs can now pat themselves on the back because of the Palestinians' efforts.

Hanna too has changed, from a man who wanted to join the Israeli system to one who is promoting a boycott of Israeli goods. But it is the Palestinian youth, he admits, who have made the uprising effective. Those who are fighting now do not have their parents' fears; they neither see the Israelis as invincible nor themselves as impotent. In fact, the twenty-year occupation has given the Palestinians an insight into the Israelis; the stability of the status quo has allowed an interchange between Arab and Jew. "The older generation was, in a way, awed by the military successes of Israel," says Hanna, "while this younger generation grew up and saw and met many Israelis." Until the present uprising his family, like many Palestinians, traveled extensively around the country. "The children feel that the Israelis are exactly like them, human beings, that they don't have a superiority over the

Palestinians. That's why today the younger generation are much more aware of their equality. They are less intimidated than the other generations. They see them as human beings with the same clay feet."

His own son, Simon, now twelve, has done a bit of rock-throwing too. Several of Simon's older friends have been arrested and the Sinioras' sixteen-year-old next-door neighbor is presently in jail. Hanna speaks with a modicum of pride of his young son's daring; and though he says that Simon has only participated "five or six times," and that his wife, Norma, "like every mother, is worried," there is a touch of boasting when he adds, "You know how it is; children have a mind of their own."

At five o'clock in the afternoon, the courtyard of the American Colony is buzzing with people. In a quiet corner, Hanna and Norma Siniora order coffee. Young Simon is about to order a Coke. "No, no," he says, changing his mind. "I'll have an R.C." Even more than their parents, Palestinian children are observing the boycott. They are careful to buy only Arab goods, and even will scold the shopkeepers who sell Israeli items.

Simon knows that his father was one of the initiators of the boycott, and is proud of his father's endeavors as a peacemaker. But Hanna has lost credibility among his peers, who see him more as a self-promoter. Even his arrests have not helped. Unlike Faisal Husseini or Radwan Abu Ayash, PLO supporters who have spent long terms in prison, Hanna has been kept only for several hours at the police headquarters in the Russian Compound. "That's good for the reputation," he says with a laugh, "but it's not enough." He knows there are many who shrug him off, and that his work is applauded more abroad than in east Jerusalem. But he will not give up his efforts. With a deep sigh he shrugs his shoulders and says, "The prophet is a heretic at home."

THE RABBI
OF DIALOGUE

A Bridge to
the Future

Rabbi Shlomo Riskin

*And the Lord spoke unto Moses, saying: "Take
the rod, and assemble the congregation, thou, and
Aaron thy brother, and speak ye unto the rock
before their eyes, that it give forth its water; and
thou shalt bring forth to them water out of the
rock; so thou shalt give the congregation and their
cattle drink." . . . And Moses lifted up his hand,
and smote the rock with his rod twice; and water
came forth abundantly, and the congregation
drank, and their cattle. And the Lord said unto
Moses and Aaron: "Because ye believed not in Me,
to sanctify Me in the eyes of the children of Israel,
therefore ye shall not bring this assembly into the
land which I have given them.*
—NUMBERS 20: 7

When Steven Riskin took his mother-in-law to the
West Bank to see the acres of dusty, barren land where
he planned to move and build a community, the

woman from New York broke out in a big smile. She returned home several days later, called Steven's mother, and told her it was the best trip she had ever made to Israel, so good that "the agent could charge me triple." She laughed as she talked about her son-in-law and daughter and how "they took me to this empty hill in no-man's-land, and they said, 'Here's going to be a synagogue, here's going to be houses, and here's going to be schools.' " But don't be concerned, she reassured Steven's mother, who was apprehensive about the move her son and his family would soon make to Israel. "It won't be in our lifetime, and it won't be in their lifetime. We have nothing to worry about."

Steven "Shlomo" Riskin is telling this story in the sleek, sand-colored living room of his modern six-bedroom house in Efrat, the settlement he started in 1981, five years after he took his mother-in-law to visit the site of his dreams. Once a vacant piece of land lying between several Arab villages, Efrat is now home to three hundred Jewish families, some of whom came to Israel to make *aliyah* with Steven Riskin when he gave up his comfortable position as orthodox rabbi of Manhattan's thriving Lincoln Square Synagogue to move here.

The forty-eight-year-old Riskin hardly fits the image of chief rabbi of the West Bank settlement; in fact, with his clean-shaven round face, his navy blue pin-striped suits bought at Barney's, his thick New York accent, and his overwhelming enthusiasm he seems more like an American salesman than an Israeli scholar. But the ritual fringes, called *tsitsis*, peeking out beneath his shirt and the yarmulke, perched on his head are telltale signs of his piety; the skill and ease with which he quotes Judaic law display his knowledge; and the ebullience and joy with which he embraces Judaism are evidence of his devotion. Short, squat, and cherubic, he walks in his own ethereal space, his arms outstretched to warmly welcome everyone, friends and strangers alike, into his personal world.

The religious community he created in the Judean Hills looks more like a well-planned American suburb than a West Bank settlement. It gleams with broad, clean streets lined with neat rows of contemporary white townhouses. Green gardens flourish in every backyard, blossoming with fruits and flowers. The town's small shopping center boasts a supermarket, an ice-cream shop, and—one of the most popular stops in the area—a pizza parlor. People on the street stop to chat, and the conversation, often about Efrat's winning baseball team, is frequently in English. (Almost half the residents come from English-speaking countries.) The street signs show colorful pictures of houses, trees, and hills, and indicate names such as "Honeybush Street," where the main synagogue, the highest building in the town, sits proudly on Pomegranate Hill overlooking the community. At the local rabbinical school, secular courses are given in subjects such as psychology and philosophy, and a special program for Ivy League schools is teaching orthodox Judaism to outstanding students.

But as similar as this may seem to a Jewish suburb on Long Island or in Los Angeles, Shlomo Riskin is well aware that this Israeli community sits amid Arab towns and close to refugee camps. Six synagogues, a leadership high school, and a rabbinical school are educating the residents in Jewish law, but the rabbi also insists that the Efrat schools teach their students Arabic. Walking along the tranquil streets, a visitor feels the immediacy of the Arab presence—in the vineyards that belong to neighboring villages, and in the minarets of the mosques jutting over the hilltops. In the distance one can hear the sound of a donkey clopping down a road through the settlement, carrying a kaffiyeh-clad Arab home to his nearby village. Once a month or so, another Arab from the same village comes to Efrat to give donkey rides, two shekels a turn, to the delighted Jewish children. Farther along, the sounds of a walkie-talkie crackle in the air, coming from a jeep that patrols the village continuously. All the men of Efrat take shifts, riding two at a time, protecting themselves with Uzi machine guns, and monitoring the area with the radio transmitters that connect them to an Israeli army base close by.

Looking out over the broad sweep of seven hills, named in the Bible for the fruits of Israel and reaching from here to Solomon's Pools, it is difficult to imagine the city of thirty thousand people that Riskin envisions for the future. For now, the Wheat and Barley and Olive hills remain empty, the population growth almost at a standstill, curtailed by the *intifada* and the fear of living too close to the Arabs. But to encourage those who might think about coming, the rabbi has built a retreat in an area of Efrat that he calls "Central Park West Bank," where English-speaking Jews can try out living in Israel on a temporary basis. He has turned at least part of his vision into reality.

Shlomo Riskin is hardly typical either of orthodox rabbis or of settlers in the occupied territories. Instead, he is an anomaly: an Israeli who lives in Judea and Samaria but insists that the Arabs around him are entitled to their own land and to sovereignty over it; an articulate scholar who quotes stories from the Bible and turns them into lessons for talking to PLO leaders such as Yasser Arafat. He meets regularly with the *mukhtars* of neighboring villages, drinks Sabbath wine made from the Arabs' vineyards, takes lessons in Arabic from local laborers, and serves as a peacemaker between arguing Arab workers. He risks his standing in his own community and among the Israeli public by taking such a liberal position; yet he jeopardizes his security by living in an area that many Israelis and virtually all Arabs consider to be not his. During the *intifada* his settlement has been fire-bombed and his car has been stoned, and he has been verbally attacked by his own family for his naivete toward the Arabs. "To be Jewish means to be in a high-risk profession," he says with a sigh. "I didn't make *aliyah* to Englewood. I made *aliyah* to Israel. That's the reality of it, a very grim reality."

Steven Riskin grew up in the turbulent Bedford-Stuyvesant section of Brooklyn, where black street gangs wielded knives and bookish Jewish boys studied hard to work their way out of the neighborhood. His parents struggled to eke out a living and placed their dreams of affluence squarely on the shoulders of their only son. Like most of their friends, they wished for their boy to grow up to be a doctor or a lawyer, and although they were not observant Jews, they sent him to the local yeshiva because its academic standards were far higher than those of the local public school. Steven's eagerness to learn about Judaism caught the attention of the yeshiva's principal, Menachem Mendel, who would take the boy home with him every Saturday afternoon to have lunch and talk about Jewish law. He would spend the rest of the Sabbath and every religious festival with his maternal grandparents, enjoying the affection of his grandmother, a devout Jew who nurtured him on the Talmud and read to him from Hebrew literature.

The combination of his school, his principal, and his grandmother had a profound influence on him. Although it badly disappointed his parents, he turned down a chance to attend Stuyvesant High School, a public school for the city's best and brightest, and chose instead the orthodox Brooklyn Talmudic Academy, where he could pursue his religious studies along with the secular curriculum. There, at the school which later became known as the Yeshiva University High School, he met Alan Dershowitz, now a famous liberal professor of law at Harvard University, and heard about another student, Meir Kahane, now the leader of the right-wing Kach party in Israel. Although

Riskin and Dershowitz were close friends and colleagues on the debating team, he and Kahane, who
was much older, did not know each other. Years later
they met when both men were active in helping Soviet
Jewry. "We never really got along," he says. At one
point, when Kahane was imprisoned but was permitted out on Friday evenings, he would eat at Riskin's house and pray in his syngagogue. "But," says
Riskin, "there were always strong ideological
clashes."

After high school Steven was offered a full scholarship to Harvard, and his parents' dream seemed
closer to fruition. But again he let them down when,
after "a moving religious experience" while saying
prayers during the festival of Sukkoth, he took an
oath to go to Yeshiva University. His last-minute announcement "disappointed my parents very much,"
he admits. "I was the great white hope—they yearned
for me to be the successful lawyer who would take
the family out of Bedford-Stuyvesant."

In the classrooms of the old Turkish-style building
in Washington Heights, he took courses in Greek and
Latin from Louis Feldman and courses in history from
Yitzhak Greenberg, two of the most demanding professors in the school. Respected by his fellow classmates for his quick mind and probing intellect, Steven
became head of the debating team and, always wearing his yarmulke, traveled around the United States
winning awards for his school. The Yeshiva campus
was a hotbed of intellectual ferment as students argued over everything, from the depiction of the Jew
in Philip Roth's novella *Goodbye Columbus*, to the
question of whether one had to believe in God to be
an orthodox Jew. The winning team argued that one
did not have to believe in God. Riskin was leader of
that team.

For Steven Riskin, who majored in the classics
and graduated summa cum laude and class valedic-
torian, opportunities abounded. His parents still cher-

ished the dream that he would go to Harvard Law School; instead he shocked them again by announcing he was going to be a rabbi. He took off for a year of study in Israel, signed up for courses at Hebrew University, and spent time with the great Jewish thinker Martin Buber. Buber's I-thou philosophy was highly appealing to an intellectual who believed so intensely in a loving God, but Buber's notion that such a God could not command laws went against the young student's convictions. "I feel very strongly about Jewish law," says Riskin, "that Jewish law has preserved us through the generations."

After two more years of study in Talmudic thought and religious law, he was ordained as a rabbi at the early age of twenty-three. But the contemplative young man was still more interested in the academic world than in the practical rabbinate; that year he became an instructor of Talmud at Yeshiva University. At the same time he started working toward his master's degree and a doctorate in Near Eastern languages and literature. "That's the ABC in a relationship," he says, "that you should be able to talk the other person's language."

When Yeshiva University received a phone call that a tiny conservative congregation in Manhattan was looking for a new rabbi, Steven Riskin, impassioned and sympathetic, was sent to meet them; his mission was to persuade them to accept an orthodox rabbi from his school. "At the end of a three-hour interview they said, 'Fine, you come.' And I said, 'I am not interested in coming.' But the more I said no, the more they said yes." Finally, after consulting with his professors, he agreed to become the rabbi, but only on his terms: because the men and women sat together, he would lead the services but would not pray; he would not take a salary, but would be allowed to teach classes and explain Judaism as he saw it; he would not move into the neighborhood but would stay in Washington Heights with his new bride,

Vicki; finally, the Lincoln Square Conservative Synagogue would change its name to Lincoln Square
Synagogue.

The twenty-four-year-old academic faced a con-
siderable challenge: to turn an apathetic laity into a
spirited congregation. Like his own parents, the
twenty-five mostly middle-aged couples and their children met only on the high holy days of Rosh Hash-
anah and Yom Kippur. They prayed three days a year
in a rented hotel room and had little other interest in
religion. Within three months the new rabbi raised
not only their consciousness but enough money to
move their meeting place to an apartment in Lincoln
Towers, near the newly completed Lincoln Center.
His enthusiasm energized the congregation; dozens of
people signed up as he formed weekly Bible and philosophy classes, created a Hebrew school, and started
Friday-night and Saturday-morning services—with
separate seating for men and women. By 1970 the
congregation had grown to five hundred families and
had settled into its own building on Sixty-Ninth Street
and Amsterdam Avenue. A year later *Time* magazine
devoted a full-page story to Steven Riskin and the
Lincoln Square Synagogue.

The rabbi's broad-minded attitudes attracted the
affluent New Yorkers, while his talent for marketing
helped draw an ever-increasing and even younger audience. His obvious love of Jewish ritual and enormous reverence for Jewish law appealed to people
looking for more meaning in their lives. His classes
on "loving and unloving"—Jewish attitudes toward
sexual ethics, marriage, and divorce—were well timed
for the 1960s sexual revolution. He empathized with
those who sought his advice about abortion and divorce and offered practical interpretations of the Talmud that addressed their needs. At a time when
abortions were illegal and many women were clam-
oring for a change in the law, he supported the
women, stating that although the rights of both the

fetus and the mother are sacred under Jewish law, the mother's rights are usually more compelling. He expressed his interest in the women's movement by doing his doctoral dissertation on the right of women to initiate divorce in Jewish law. But perhaps even more important, to assimilated Jews caught up in the frenzy of ambition, he was able to impart his appreciation of the strict laws of the Sabbath, the one day of the week when work must be set aside, telephone calls must go unheeded, taxicabs and buses must remain unhailed, and home and the family become the focus of attention.

The city of Efrat lies eight miles south of Jerusalem, part of an area called Gush Etzion, a block of land bought by Jews from the Arabs in 1928, on which they built four kibbutzim that flourished until the birth of the Jewish state. For five months prior to the Israeli War of Independence, the people of Etzion were under seige; and on May 11, 1948, with Arab attacks coming closer, the children of the villages were evacuated. The next day, only forty-eight hours before the state of Israel was proclaimed, the Arab Legion massacred 148 of the 152 people who remained to defend the area.

Moshe Moshovicz had grown up in Etzion and had been on a special mission in Cyprus when his family and their home were destroyed. For nineteen years afterward the land belonged to Jordan, but in 1967, when the Israelis captured the West Bank, Moshe joined the other surviving children and paid a visit to the area. With their hearts still aching for those they had lost, they swore that someday they would rebuild the Jewish community.

Nine years later, in 1976, Moshe met Steven Riskin, the American rabbi who was on a visit to Israel, and became enamored with his enthusiasm and creative vision. He invited Riskin to take a ride with him, and together they drove along the road toward Hebron until the Israeli stopped the car. As Riskin looked around, all that he could see was bare, parched land studded with boulders and tufts of desert grass. But Moshovicz pointed toward the empty hill and told the rabbi the story of his family. "I have a dream to build a city for Gush Etzion and to call it Efrat," Riskin remembers him saying. "But I need a partner. If you'll be my partner, with God's help, you'll be the rabbi and I'll be the mayor."

For Riskin, to be a serious Jew and not to live in Israel was almost irreconcilable, yet he was highly regarded and content as leader of the dynamic New York City congregation. He had wrestled with the notion of giving it up to move to Israel but had never found the right opportunity. Now, listening to Moshe, "I really believed it could happen," he says, his voice still filled with the determination that Moshovicz sensed. "We shook hands and he and I began to actively plan for Efrat." Back in the United States Riskin talked excitedly about the project and organized a group of followers called Raishit Geulah, "The Beginning of Redemption." Someday, he hoped, they would come to Efrat with him.

Although Steven was still the rabbi at the Lincoln Square Synagogue, the Riskins and their four children spent the next five summers living in Israel. During the days he worked on a kibbutz, then spent time meeting with Israeli officials to develop Efrat, etching a city out of the dry brown hill and carving a career for himself near the biblical site of the Book of Ruth. At the time, he says, none of the land that the government granted him was confiscated from the Arabs, because no one had been living there for nearly two thousand years. "This was really the cradle of the Jewish people. I don't think I have the right to displace anyone who is living anywhere. But if no one is living there, and if I have my roots there, of course I have a right to be there." Furthermore, the Israeli high court decreed that the vineyards that local Arabs had recently begun cultivating should remain in the ownership of the Arabs. "Therefore," he is quick to say, "I am not a settler, I am a citizen; and I am not an occupier, I am a resident."

When the Riskins were ready to move to Efrat, two hundred families were eager to go with them. They were told they could have new houses with small down payments and low interest rates, and that jobs would be readily available. But by the time they actually applied for the mortgages, the funds had dried up and the homes that were supposed to cost forty thousand dollars actually cost one hundred thousand dollars. Jobs turned out to be scarce, and life in Israel seemed too unmanageable to many of the prosperous New Yorkers. In the end, however, 115 families did make *aliyah*, but only 25 came to Efrat. When Riskin did not produce as many Americans as he had promised, a number of Israelis who had agreed to settle in the community became angry and skeptical of his word. In his typically positive way, Riskin speaks proudly about the families who did come and those who followed later, and talks optimistically of those who are still making plans to come.

The long-bearded orthodox rabbis of Jerusalem were not about to make it easy for the smooth-faced American, especially one who had permitted his daughter to enter the army, to become one of their own. His intellectual open-mindedness and his unconventional thinking threatened their traditional approach. When Riskin applied for permission to join the Israeli rabbinate, they grilled him for an hour and forty minutes in an oral exam, asking obscure Talmudic questions, hoping to trip him up on some arcane bit of knowledge. "Thank God, I did okay," he says, "but they really tried." At his installation as rabbi of the city of Efrat, Steven Riskin, now called by his Hebrew name, Shlomo, lived up to his liberal reputation and celebrated with a show of West Bank solidarity. As a guest speaker at the ceremony, he invited the *mukhtar* of the nearby Arab village of Beit Fajar.

The road from Jerusalem to Efrat passes by Dehaishe, one of the most seething refugee camps in the West Bank. Long before the *intifada*, youths raised in this boiling pot of hatred hurled rocks and stones at Israeli soldiers, and several times in recent months the rabbi's car, like others with yellow Israeli license plates, has been attacked. Many who drive by the camp turn their heads, trying not to see the cramped rows of ugly concrete huts mired in stench and barricaded behind barbed wire. But Shlomo Riskin refuses to ignore their existence. "I usually look at it very carefully," he says as he rides by on the way home with his guests. "I believe as a Jew that my tradition commands me to reach out to every human being. There is no one that I can look at and not see, listen to and not hear. There can't be invisible people."

Soon after Efrat was established, the rabbi arranged to meet with several *mukhtars* of the nearby Arab villages to discuss the problems of Dehaishe. "The very first order of business in terms of Jewish-Arab relations must be to erase those refugee camps. We cannot be responsible for people who live like that, and if the United Nations refuses to allow us to do anything, if Arab states refuse to allow us to do anything, then we have to do it on our own."

Even more importantly, the rabbi wanted to begin a dialogue with the Arab leaders. "I believe we have different kinds of relationships. Not every relationship can be an I-thou, Buberian relationship," he says. There must also be I-you relationships and even, he is somewhat reluctant to admit, I-it relationships with people like the postman and the taxi driver. But Riskin firmly believes that "you have to have a number of I-thou relationships with people who are not exactly like you. In terms of the Arab world, that was very important."

The first gathering was held in the elaborate home of the *mukhtar* of Ramallah, where friendly conversation took place over fruit juice and, in respect for the guest of honor, kosher cookies. Although the problems of the refugee camp were not resolved, an important relationship was started between the heads of the communities; the rabbi left with a large bag of pistachio nuts, freshly picked from the *mukhtar*'s garden, a gift of friendship and hope. The return visit was at the Riskins' home, where, in respect for the Arab tradition, cold drinks, fresh fruit, and cakes were served to the guests. The rabbi watched in awe as one *mukhtar* gobbled slice after slice of homemade cake. "He was half my size and he ate fifteen slices of cake," Shlomo says with a smile. "He wanted to be nice to me, to show me that he liked my hospitality."

While they relaxed on leather sofas in the living room that overlooks the Judean Hills, Riskin proposed that the group develop a concrete idea that they could work on together. Out of the discussion emerged the possibility of a joint medical clinic, an innovative concept that hints at the potential relationship he visualizes. The nonprofit clinic would be built on vacant land just outside Efrat. It would be sponsored by private donations, mostly from Americans, and would be staffed by equal numbers of Jewish and Arab doctors. Although some residents of Efrat objected to the idea, most viewed it as constructive and even welcomed it with enthusiasm. Over the course of several more meetings, the notion grew into a well-formed plan; Riskin was ready to present it to the American ambassador in Israel and had even invited one of the *mukhtars* to join him on a fund-raising trip to the United States. But the outbreak of the *intifada* put a halt to the meetings: Arab extremists have threatened and even murdered other Arabs who cooperate with Israelis, and so the efforts of both sides have been, at least temporarily, put aside. But Shlomo

Riskin still holds out the hope that the cooperative clinic will come into being.

Quietly now, the rabbi still meets with the *mukhtar* of another nearby village. The hamlet of Wadi Nes has grown from just a few houses to eighty families, thriving in the wake of the burgeoning Jewish settlement and even receiving its water from Efrat. Its men earn substantial incomes helping to build the homes and synagogues of Efrat, working in its stores, and cultivating the vineyards that dot the landscape. The symbiotic relationship between the neighboring Arabs and Jews has been a positive example of West Bank harmony, and even in the turmoil of the *intifada*, the Palestinians continue to come to work and the Israelis continue to supply them with water.

Recently, when an Arab woman from Wadi Nes was stricken with a heart attack, the *mukhtar* brought her to Riskin's house. The rabbi called the local Jewish doctor who came within five minutes and took care of the patient. The Arab shook the rabbi's hand and told him how grateful he was. But then he shook his head and asked, "When are you going to stop the water?"

"Why should I stop the water?" Shlomo replied.

"Well, now our people are fighting," said the *mukhtar*.

"But *our* people are not fighting," answered the rabbi.

The road to Wadi Nes runs directly through Efrat, and although few who live in the small village own cars, once in a while an Arab can be seen driving through the Jewish town. Until recently, no one in Efrat gave much thought to the blue license-plated cars, but in the surge of the uprising, their presence has become a perceived danger. No stones have yet been thrown, no Molotov cocktails have been tossed from a car window, yet the Jewish residents know that an Arab terrorist hiding gasoline bombs in his vehicle could easily drive through their town, telling the guard patrols who might stop him at the entrance that he was simply on his way to Wadi Nes.

At six o'clock on a summer morning, several residents of Efrat, frightened by the thought of such an attack, blocked the road to Wadi Nes with heavy stones. When the *mukhtar* was informed about the roadblock he rushed to see the rabbi, pleading that the stones be removed. Shlomo Riskin agreed with his Arab neighbor that the road should remain open, but the community of Efrat was divided. The Israelis recognized that by the act of closing the road they were condemning the Palestinians. But if they left it open, they left themselves vulnerable. "It's a complex issue," Riskin says. "The people of Wadi Nes have been so nice, even though there's extra risk involved, we can't repay their niceness with harshness." Heated debate followed for an hour until the Israelis' city council voted to remove the stones. Nevertheless, many of the residents, and even members of Riskin's own family, disagree with the rabbi: they recall an earlier incident that disproved his theories of dialogue and friendship.

From the earliest days of his arrival as a citizen in Israel, Shlomo Riskin was determined to establish relationships with those who lived around him. One of the first goals he set for himself was to speak Arabic. "When you learn the other person's language, what you're also saying is, the other person has a nation, the other person has a culture, the other person has a tradition." He suggested the idea to a young Arab who worked at the Efrat supermarket. The twenty-three-year-old Majid, who spoke fluent English and Hebrew, not only agreed to be Riskin's tutor, but even refused to be paid. Instead, and only at the rabbi's insistence, Majid would accept a music tape or other gift that Riskin would bring back from his trips to the United States. The bond between the two men grew, and Shlomo says, "I believed we became very friendly." At one point, when a brother of Majid lost his job because of problems with his Israeli documents, Shlomo stepped in and helped him get his job back.

Student and teacher would meet several times a week, frequently on Friday afternoons at the rabbi's house when his teenaged daughter and sons were often at home. "My family was not always so crazy about this," he admits in something of an understatement. But when his wife argued angrily, he would answer just as emotionally, "These are my neighbors. We let Jews in; we have to let Arabs in. And I want my children to see that, too."

But then one afternoon, he says, "something very sad happened": A gasoline bomb exploded at the busy bus stop just outside Efrat. Moments before the explosion Majid had been seen "monkeying around" at the scene of the crime. Later on he was taken in by the police and questioned as the chief suspect, but no charges were ever filed against him. Nevertheless, says the rabbi, still shaken by the incident, the young Arab never returned. "To my mind it's important that he never spoke to me afterward. I never saw him, never spoke to him. He never came back to Efrat again." Shlomo's children told him they hoped he had learned his lesson. But the rabbi still holds firmly to his belief in the importance of human ties. "There could be ten Majids," he told them, "but that's how I have to act. I can't live differently."

The tenuous relationship between Arab and Jew became clear to him once again this summer when he took his customary morning jog on a road that goes past his house to the stone quarries beyond Efrat. As he jogged, Shlomo noticed a shepherd in the fields with his flock and paid little attention to the man. But his nonchalance disappeared when he saw the Arab pick up two stones. The rabbi immediately felt frightened, aware that during the midst of the *intifada* he was alone and vulnerable in no-man's-land. Just as quickly, however, he realized that the shepherd had picked up the stones for his own defense; he too was scared, fearful that the Israeli might throw something at him. "I started to cry," says Shlomo sadly. "We're afraid of each other. That's the tragedy of this kind of situation."

On a Friday afternoon the telephone in his house is ringing nonstop as the rabbi juggles a discussion of orthodox Judaism with phone calls about fund raising, calls about religious ceremonies, and calls about his neighbors' personal problems. Only the coming of sundown will suspend the ringing. Every other minute, it seems, he is jumping up from the low-slung sofa and dashing across the marble floors to grab the receiver. "For me the blessing of the Sabbath is that there is no phone," he says with a sigh. "I can truly rest. I can be with my family."

He welcomes the Sabbath with a shower and a new set of clothes and covers his yarmulke with a gray felt hat while his wife completes the preparations for the evening celebration. She has already baked the *challah* bread and cooked the gefilte fish that start off every Friday-night meal. Before sundown she must finish the cooking and have the table fully set. She drapes it with a white cloth and places three candelabras, one for her and each of their daughters, in a row. "I love the traditions," says Shlomo. "I love the rituals. I think they have very real, very meaningful messages to give forth."

On the way to early evening services, he exults over the events that took place in the synagogue the week before: the circumcision of an eight-day-old boy, performed while he held the baby on his lap; the announcements by two different people of the births of baby girls; the bar mitzvah of a thirteen-year-old boy; and the news that one couple in the community had become engaged. "For each joyous occasion, there was spontaneous singing from the congregation. There's a very warm feeling here," he says with pride.

Strolling along the streets he helped create, his fedora crowning his head, he is king of his world, greeting everyone he sees with a warm grin and an enthusiastic *"Shabbat shalom."*

For him, Efrat is proof of the beginning of redemption. "There's a beautiful passage that says the redemption will come just like the dawn—stage by stage, little by little. It may even come with setbacks. Miraculous things have happened in our generation: after two thousand years, the return to Israel of all the exiles, including the Ethopian exiles. It's amazing. It's very heartwarming and very exciting and thrilling to live in Israel at this period. For me to see Efrat, a city, spring up from my five fingers is a very exciting feeling."

At home with his two sons, Hillel and Yoni, aged thirteen and fifteen; his daughter Elana, twenty-one; and his wife, Vicki, he removes his coat and slips on a silky jacquard robe. Only his older daughter, Batya, who is welcoming Shabbat with her own husband and year-old baby just a few blocks away, is missing from the family portrait. Tonight the children will serve the meal while mother and father relax for the Sabbath. The Riskins take their places at the long dining-room table as husband and wife, holding hands and sitting side by side at the head. Then they chant the prayers over the candles, the bread, and the wine. Shlomo snaps his fingers with joy and sways his arms to the rhythm as he leads the others in singing the traditional Sabbath songs welcoming the Sabbath bride, praising the Jewish wife. Taking a sip of the sweet red wine, his face beams as he proudly notes it was made from the grapes of Arab-owned vineyards, given as a gift to the family.

But his exaltation is deflated somewhat during a discussion about Jewish fundamentalists like Meir Kahane, who want to drive the Arabs out of the territories. This is an attitude, he says, that "Judaism has never sanctioned. That extremist position, I think, leads to dangerous things. We have to temper what's happening with a sensitivity toward the stranger. I think the model of the whole exodus from Egypt and how the Bible commands us to treat the Egyptians—'You must love the Egyptian because you were a stranger in his land'—these are critical models for us." He sips some of the vegetable soup and continues, "They have a right to have their land on which they live. I have no problem with that at all."

While the family enjoys a dinner of sesame chicken, rice, salad, and stewed tomatoes, father and son tangle over Shlomo's liberal stand. He has heard his son before, arguing from a pro-Kahane position, but he has also heard his son ask someone to leave the house because the person used disrespectful language about an Arab. Shlomo's irritation with the extremists is challenged by his boy, who reminds him that although most who live in Efrat agree with him, a significant percentage of the community follows Kahane. Shlomo pushes this notion aside with a wave of his hand and mentions that many in Efrat are supporters of the liberal group Peace Now. But the reality of the pro-Kach presence does not go unnoticed; Riskin may have created the community, and he has the support of most of its citizens, but he still must face the wrath of many who live here.

Nevertheless he argues openly and intensely for a dialogue with the Palestinians and urges the Israeli government to talk to the PLO. He uses the vernacular of the Palestinians when he speaks about their problems and insists that they should have a homeland in the West Bank, even with a capital in east Jerusalem.

"I think every nation requires independence and a sense of independence—a sense of running its own affairs. It's the right of every nation state to have its flag flying, to have a sense that it elects its own government heads. That's part of one's self-image."

As his son squirms in his chair and looks doubtfully at his father, Shlomo reminds him of the biblical story of Moses and the rock. As the Jewish people were crying of thirst in the desert, God told Moses to take a staff and to hold it, but not to use it to hit the rock. Speak to the rock, God told him. Do not hit it. And water will come out. But Moses disobeyed and hit the rock twice. Water came out, but Moses was punished for his action and was not allowed to enter the Promised Land.

For centuries Jewish scholars have debated the reason that Moses was punished. Riskin believes that the story is a lesson in the power of speech. "All relationships begin and end with proper communication. I believe the message is very clear. God said to the Jewish people when they were up against a rock, 'You've got to speak to the rock. And if you speak to it and you learn to speak properly, then water can even come out of a rock.' "

Putting the story in terms of the present situation, he says, "You have to be willing to speak to those people who sometimes seem as hard-hearted to us as rocks. We've got to be willing to speak to anybody. Even to the rock. Even to people like Yasser Arafat or the Hizballah. I would speak to anybody."

Perhaps out of that dialogue between Palestinians and Israelis can come the harmony and peaceful co-operation that Shlomo Riskin envisions.

ACKNOWLEDGMENTS

We want to thank the many Arabs and Israelis who helped us. Palestinian journalists Ziad Abu Zayyad, Said al-Ghazali, Radwan Abu Ayash, and Jan Abu Shakra of the Palestine Human Rights Committee were invaluable in helping us establish contacts. Our thanks also to Ibrahim Dakkak, Darwish Nasser, and Sari Nuseibeh for their wisdom and guidance.

We want to stress our gratitude to Danny Rubinstein of *Davar*, who read and reread, analyzed, and criticized every page, forcing us to write many more drafts than we had originally contemplated.

We are indebted to Avi Pazner and Yoram Elron of the Israeli Government. Yehoshafat Harkabi of Hebrew University and Abdul Latif Barghouti of Bir Zeit University were invaluable in helping us understand the history of the struggle. Our special thanks also to Ari Rath, editor-in-chief of the *Jerusalem Post*, and the staff at *Al-Fajr*. Yael Amzalek and the kind people at Mishkenot Sha'ananim provided a tranquil setting for us to write the book after returning from the turbulent West Bank and Gaza.

We are grateful to Marie Arana-Ward, our editor, for embracing this book, and to Elizabeth Harper for helping us to see it through. Geoffrey Kemp of the Carnegie Endowment for International Peace and Samuel Lewis, former U.S. Ambassador to Israel, gave us criticism and support when we needed it most. Olivier Raffet was always at our side taking sensitive photographs.

But most of all, we could not have completed this project without Deborah Wilgoren and the generosity of the Rockefeller Center for Social Sciences at Dartmouth College. Debbie's tireless efforts transcribing dozens of interviews and researching the complex histories were essential to the project. Her sense of humor and patience with us at trying moments will always be remembered.

DATE DUE			